# By Demonstration: God

# By Demonstration: God

*Fifty Years and a Week at L'Abri*

**Wade Bradshaw**

Piquant Editions is a registered company in England and
    Wales (No. 5093557).
Registered office: 4 Thornton Road, Carlisle, CA3 9HZ, UK
E-mail: info@piquant.net
Website: www.piquant.net

ISBN 1-903689-33-3

A catalogue record of this book is available in the UK
    from the British Library

Cover design by Projectluz
Cover photographs copyright © 2004 by Wade Bradshaw
    and Tricia Porter
Book design by www.2aT.com

# Contents

# Foreword

Half a century ago, a small, wiry man with an extraordinary vision and his beautiful and equally far-sighted wife together founded the L'Abri Fellowship. As so often happens in life, Francis and Edith Schaeffer had no idea what the profound repercussions of that act of obedient faith would be. The establishment of L'Abri is undoubtedly Francis Schaeffer's greatest achievement. He has been listed, with John Stott, James I Packer and C S Lewis, among the foremost shapers of American evangelicalism since the Second World War. As a superb communicator, teacher and mentor, with extraordinary pastoral gifts and ability to empathize, he influenced the lives of countless people throughout the world.

The work and achievement of L'Abri are very difficult to categorize, itemize and rationalize. 'The Shelter' is organic rather than mechanistic, growing and taking shape according to the people who turn up to study there and the people who are there to lead and teach and mentor them, but held together by energetic and creative exposition of biblical truth. (I can hear Schaeffer's words ringing: 'God has an infinite imagination.') After he died in 1984, the family-shaped organization he left behind had to develop its own identity. Its new leaders were willing to wind it up if that was the right thing to do—but today it remains one of the most vital Christian ministries in the world (thankfully, not measured by size).

Francis Schaeffer hated hagiography and I think he would have liked the affectionate but honest account Wade Bradshaw gives of L'Abri. It takes the form of engaging meditations based on the daily, and even hourly, life of the English fellowship, where the days of the week are almost like seasons, with distinctive activities that give structure and coherence to the often vulnerable human lives that form the community—a community short-lived for some but more permanent for others.

*By Demonstration: God*

It is not a monastic community, like those of the early Middle Ages that helped to preserve civilization at a time when the future looked exceedingly bleak. Rather, it is a pilot community, inspired by Jesus' teaching about the Kingdom of God, which gives tantalizing hints of proper human living in the world today, and where God is working in constantly surprising ways. The style of living that it signals is not just a beautiful dream but something that is real, faithful and true, that brings substantial healing in our fractured lives. I found these clues at L'Abri as a young man in the experimental world of the late 1960s, and I still see them in L'Abri today in the very different (and yet not so different) world of the early 21st century.

Colin Duriez*

---

*Colin Duriez studied under Francis Schaeffer at L'Abri in Switzerland during the late 1960s. At present he is a freelance writer, editor and publishing consultant. His published works include *The C. S. Lewis Encyclopedia*, *The Poetic Bible*, *The Inklings Handbook*, *Tolkien and 'The Lord of the Rings'*, *J.R.R. Tolkien and C.S. Lewis: The Story of Their Friendship*, and *A Field Guide to Narnia*. He also edited 'God's Hand in History' in volume 6 of *The Complete Works of Hans Rookmaaker*.

# What Has Been and What Shall Be

*"To show forth by demonstration, in our lives and work, the existence of God"*

People who have never visited a branch of L'Abri ask what it is, what they are, what we do—they find it difficult to formulate the proper question. And in this we share common ground, because for those of us who have lived and worked at L'Abri, even those who have been part of the fellowship for a long time, it's difficult to formulate just the right answer. Anything brief enough to keep the interest of the questioner is going to leave them with misconceptions.

> Oh, it's like a school.
>
> So, it's a retreat centre.
>
> Sounds like a commune, then.
>
> Ah, I see, you're a missionary.

Some of these answers are more accurate than others, but none of them even begins to capture the spirit of this creature called L'Abri Fellowship. And here we are, 50 years on from its very small family beginnings, and there is still no sharper definition. This is partly by design, partly by accident, but it is almost always a problem. Immigration officers in the countries where

L'Abri has branches frown and think about summoning their managers after they've asked someone coming to visit us for a description. Children whose parents work in L'Abri never quite know what to say when their friends ask them what their folks do for a living. (I've heard that to avoid that conversation one child simply took to saying that his father worked at Ford.) And our neighbours are frequently just as clueless. All they know for sure is that someone who looks slightly scruffy and jet-lagged, on foot with a backpack or dragging a suitcase down the pavement, usually needs directions to L'Abri.

In the village near the English branch many people consider us a cult and some call us 'the house of prayer'—but my favourite description I heard one night in the pub. No one at the bar knew that I lived at L'Abri when talk turned to whatever it was that went on in the rambling manor house down at the other end of the village. Several fascinating theories were advanced, and then a man said with confidence, as if to settle the matter: 'Those are the loonies who dance in a circle.' I still have no idea what he meant, except that it revealed that we have a local image problem. I do recall one lovely summer evening when two Russian students living with us treated us to a Russian meal and a Russian film, and then took about 40 of us out onto the lawn to teach us Russian folk dancing and laugh at us when we couldn't do it. We were in a big circle. Maybe this neighbour was out walking his dog and saw us as the night fell gently.

There are currently eight branches of L'Abri, in seven countries and on three continents—residential centres where people come to live and study with us. Each branch is different from all the others. They differ primarily because they have different people working and living there. However, they also vary because each is surrounded by a different culture and situation. Also, different people arrive at the various front doors and they bring with them things they wish to discuss, varying issues to wrestle with. The same question—even the same words—become a new question, new words, because spoken by a different person. We all share the same world but we also all labour within a different story. We are a community made of individuals.

There are many differences; and yet, despite the commitment to being free to demonstrate God's existence in our lives and work differently, we share many things as well. We have a common heritage through the work of Francis and Edith Schaeffer, who began the work with an open home in post-war Switzerland. We have a common commitment to the Bible as the true message from the Creator God through his prophets and apostles. And we all believe—and try to live as if we believe—that this God still does stuff: that he continues to listen to his children and answer their prayers. We remain curious and hopeful—both of which can look unusual in a cynical, disappointed age. We think that the Christian message, because it is true, has something to say, some implication for every aspect of human endeavour: all our arts and sciences, all our relationships. We think that men and women are in the image of God, and therefore very valuable and very interesting both as individuals and as a species. We find that we are living in a world fallen into alienation from its Creator, in a cosmos that groans beneath its frustration and its bondage to decay. We are interested in education but think that actually the answer to our ills is redemption through faith and obedience to the gospel of Jesus Christ.

And so we live at L'Abri. It is just a tiny part of the Church, the supernatural family through time and geography.

All of the various branches do things differently, but there is a resemblance between us even across the continents. We have similar purposes, similar methods and similar rhythms. How, then, to communicate the differences and the similarities? That is the first challenge facing this book. Its structure follows the weekly schedule of the English branch because it would be misleading to try to discuss L'Abri outside of a very particular setting. And yet the various parts of the week will differ between the branches. This is the answer to the first challenge, a fair introduction to L'Abri: to insist on being particular, while also admitting diversity and remaining slightly unpredictable.

The second challenge is more serious and more subtle. Over the past 50 years, thousands of people have wandered through the different L'Abri communities. No one could begin to guess accurately how many have studied with us, how many meals have been served, how many conversations or conversions have occurred. We have many good friends who remember us fondly and wish us well. They might happily read a book reflecting on God's faithfulness to L'Abri over the past half century. That would be a good tale, and we should practise gratitude by rehearsing again the mighty deeds of God among us. But the second challenge facing this book is that, even in its thankful reflections, it must keep its face turned to the future. How, then, to avoid nostalgia and self-congratulation?

The answer to this second challenge is probably much like that given in the scriptures. We are to remind ourselves of God's generosity and his judgements in the past. We are to set our hopes in the revelation of the bright future, when the good shall finally overcome and destroy all that is evil, when the universe shall be frustrated no longer and all groaning shall cease, the bondage broken. This recounting of the past and this longing for the future are both meant in the Church's life to be in evidence in the present day, in this very moment.

We have no other moment than the one we find ourselves in: it is no good wishing things otherwise. However, this does not dismiss history to the bin of irrelevance. One of the first things I learned from L'Abri was the importance of history. Somehow, perhaps because I came from the optimism of the New World, I had lived with an unexamined assumption. I knew history after a fashion, and yet I actually lived as if things in the world had always been pretty much as I experienced them. I should have remembered otherwise. I should have remembered the shock I had the first time I was ill enough to stay home from school. Up to that day I had thought that the world was my story: that while I was gone to Grady Elementary everything stood still awaiting my return, everyone leaned against the wall and smoked cigarettes like movie extras waiting for the star to arrive for the next scene. I was shocked when I realized—when I really had to face the fact—that the world went on even though I wasn't there watching and benefiting: the postman came, the daytime soap operas played, the drug store did steady business.

It is even so with history. Things have not always been as they are now. And, though it is a very complicated tale, we can learn how things have come to be as we experience them. Far from being irrelevant, this tale of time is worth knowing, not least of all if we are dissatisfied with how things are and wish to see them change.

And the future has its role in the present even as the past does. Hope seems always to have some relationship to an imagined future, and human beings never flourish without hope: they wither away. Christianity has always dwelt on its future hope—enough so, in fact, that its critics have at times made the mistake of saying that it does not contribute to its day. What is easily lost in the debate is the truth that knowledge of the future hope can actually free a Christian believer to be of greater service in the present. If one is assured that fulfilment is coming, one can live for the benefit of others.

And so this book will try to allow the past and the future to have their proper say in the present moment.

# At the Door with the Broken Sign

*"It is not because there is no one to speak with that men are lonely but because they are cut off from the One who can fulfil their loneliness."*
Francis Schaeffer

L'Abri Fellowship is 50 years old in 2005. It began as a family offering hospitality to visitors, hospitality and conversation about spiritual issues. It was as simple and as complicated as a large family of big personalities sharing their lives with their guests. Over the years, the guests became students and others came to join with the family: working in the community, listening to the students, trying to answer their questions honestly and faithfully. People were impressed, impressed by how coherent the ideas were, impressed by the way they were clearly acted out in everyday situations. Prayer seemed less of a luxury and more of an absolute necessity. What began in a faithful obscurity got 'extruded' into prominence. Books were written; film series were made.

This growth and a sort of success were an encouragement, of course, and a cause of joy, but they also brought predictable tensions. Once L'Abri had outgrown its family roots, how could it retain its vitality? Doesn't the life drain out of something beautiful when it begins the inevitable process of becoming an institution? This is a strain, to remain vital; but it is a struggle that everyone faces every day and in every relationship. It is no good trying to achieve vitality by jettisoning everything from your life as it becomes familiar and habit-ridden. Every church, every school, every marriage, every government has to ask if it is still living according to its principles, or has reality given way to merely protecting an image?

Hospitality has remained important at L'Abri. (The words *l'abri* simply mean 'the shelter' in French.) People arrive at odd hours and with strange needs. They come for many reasons and by many avenues. It was my South African colleague Jock MacGregor, who now lives at the Minnesota branch of L'Abri, who first alerted me to this. I remember that we were having high tea in Jock and Alison's home: a fire crackled in the grate behind me, there were lots of people sitting around the room and I was on the floor. Jock was welcoming a new group of us that had just arrived. We didn't know one another yet, and the atmosphere in that room was a mixture of anticipation and discomfort. He remarked to us very casually, but in a way that has remained with me for over a decade, that the question 'How did you come to be at L'Abri?' is much more than a polite ice-breaker and a social convention. Over the years he had observed that it is another way of asking: 'How did God bring you to be at this place at this time?'

This is because the community doesn't advertise its existence. (We argued for a long time about whether it was appropriate for us even to have a website.) Instead of recruiting visitors, the community prays that the Living God will bring the right people in need of shelter of various kinds, and it continues to pray that God will keep people away for whom it is not the right time for a visit. This is also the reason why the story of L'Abri has to be told through the stories of people. Each arrival is an answered prayer, full of danger and potential. Some of the stories are dramatic, while others are very ordinary; but every time the front door opens and there is a new person, slightly unsure of what is going on at this big house, something very important is happening.

There is a sweeping gravel driveway leading up to an oval of grass in the front. The house is beautiful but it is also intimidating: bristling with chimneys, it looks like some great man-of-war stranded heavily by the tide. On the oval a tired-looking bicycle rests on its side and a yellow dog sleeps in the sun. The house would be harder to approach were it not for these signs of relaxed family life. This must be the place, but you aren't entirely sure because you're fatigued. You have been travelling all day, perhaps you are jet-lagged, the train was late and your luggage grew heavy in the walk from the station.

There is an arch over the entranceway over which a wisteria blooms exuberantly, and in its shadow you can just make out a sign on the big oak door. The sign has a crack tracing diagonally all the way across its face, but at least this is the right place. You knock on the door, but you hardly make a sound: they don't make doors this way any more. It is thick and solid. There is no bell. Maybe you should just wait? In the edginess of the moment you wonder if maybe you shouldn't have come at all. It occurs to you that this was all someone else's idea: someone else had suggested that you would like to study at this place, study all those questions that had been nagging you and that no one seemed to have the time or inclination to take seriously. It had seemed such a good idea back then, but now you're not so sure.

You hear voices on the other side of the door. You can't quite make them out—it might be a child squealing. You knock again, but no one can hear you. In frustration, you try the heavy handle and find that the door is open. It swings inwards easily, and there is someone reading in a chair just inside, someone you've never met before. They look very comfortable to you, and very at home in these surroundings. It will be several days before you discover they had only arrived two days earlier.

Maggie Curry is the granddaughter of the couple who founded L'Abri. She and her husband, Doug, worked in rural Nepal for many years before they returned to live and work at L'Abri in England. At the 50th anniversary of the Fellowship her family is now busy with its own adventure of beginning a new branch on Bowen Island, off the west coast of Canada. Maggie told me the story of the arrival of a woman at the door to our big house. Fiona was one of those who turned that heavy handle and entered. She arrived at L'Abri with only the one little bag she had toted all around Central Europe for the past few months. The same bag she had packed to leave home right after her 18th birthday. 'Prague was everything I thought I wanted,' she told Maggie. 'It was beautiful. I had no responsibilities. I could do whatever I wished.' However, Fiona's sister had always kept her strong faith in Christ, and she was concerned for her wandering sibling. It was this sister who had mentioned L'Abri as a place she could go and stay at on her trek through Europe. 'I was always kind of jealous of my sister,' Fiona admitted to Maggie, who was acting as her tutor during her stay, 'but I thought I wasn't the sort of person who could ever have her kind of belief. When I got to the Czech Republic I didn't know if I was a Christian or not, but I'd given up on practising my faith.'

In a tiny cement apartment, which had become an oven in the August heat of Prague, Fiona got talking to another young traveller. During their conversation the name of Jesus was mentioned, and Fiona replied comfortably, 'I don't really feel Jesus is relevant to me at all.'

'Well, then,' the young man observed, 'you can't call yourself a Christian.'

Fiona was stunned to realize that he was right. 'It never struck me before that the whole Jesus thing was actually necessary.'

Later, travelling in England, on an impulse she spontaneously joined a group of Anglican vicars who invited her to fill a vacant seat aboard their tour bus, and wound up in London with them. That same day she took the train from Waterloo Station to the town of Liss. She walked the last two miles along a winding country road and found L'Abri. There was the oval with its bicycle and its dog.

'I'm not sure what I thought I would accomplish by a visit to L'Abri,' she explained. 'Only, I knew I needed to talk to somebody about God. I think now that I wanted to have penetrating conversations without revealing anything about myself.' She stood outside the door and heard voices inside the Manor House. She swung her bag over her shoulder, gave the door a push and went in.

There was music playing in the Victorian kitchen at the back. Someone blonde called Petra (who turned out to be another student and who would become a good friend) was stirring an enormous pot of spaghetti on a small stove. People were laughing, and a three-year-old was bouncing around in the hallway on a big rubber ball. 'I had no idea about anything at L'Abri,' Fiona remembers. 'What on earth had I come to? Who were these people?' Whatever she had come to, one thing was abundantly obvious: she was in the midst of someone's home. Back in the days before most bookings to L'Abri were done by e-mail, we would answer every query with a handwritten letter and a copy of an introductory brochure. I have always appreciated the words of that brochure, which forewarned visitors that 'Children and pets are much in evidence.' It's all so unusual and at the same time so unremarkable and ordinary.

Francis and Edith Schaeffer began L'Abri as a way of life rather than as a job, but even for them the arrival was not easy. They had four children with them while they worked as missionaries in post-war Switzerland, when they decided to leave the comparative security of their mission agency and set off on a new adventure more reliant on God's guidance and provision. They had no plan or programme to follow but desired to live a life that demonstrated God's reality and his ongoing interaction with the world of his creatures. The Schaeffers longed that anyone who came to stay with them would be able to ask their real questions without fear of criticism.

'I felt very quickly after I arrived that I could be open about my own position and my own view of Christianity,' a student named Angus told Doug Curry. 'I thought I had come to L'Abri, but I found I was being met where I was rather than being pushed to conform to the norms that you'd find in church. I could be quite vocal about my criticisms of Christianity without anyone taking it personally.'

A tour of the big red manor house is given to all newcomers, though it's hard to take it all in on the first day. Edith Reitsema, a Dutch woman who spent much of her childhood in the townships of South Africa, is usually the guide. She is very busy, because she dislikes taking groups round because that would contribute to 'an institutional feel' to our life together. She much prefers taking people round individually so she can answer their unique concerns about coming to this new and difficult-to-describe place. Just the layout of the property is confusing. One room gives way to the next. The study room, with its row of desks and subdued afternoon sunlight, the library full of tattered books and equally well-worn sofas, the living room—which isn't the same thing as the high-ceilinged breakfast room—the office, various flats, the Bake House, the gardens, the chapel, the Pump House. Edith herself lives in the Well House, a small flat she has turned into a beautiful home. Along one wall she has made curtains for the long row of windows from a material of a rich dark blue. She bought 30 metres of the stuff from an outdoor market in Utrecht. The poor trader, used to getting his way with customers, after bargaining for a while with this woman who looks European but haggles like an African, finally surrendered—and then asked her where she was from.

And then there are all the faces and names and accents along the tour and during the first few days: at every corner we turn there seems to be another person vacuuming a floor or chopping tomatoes or reading and taking notes. Edith understands your bewilderment and tells you that there is only one thing really to remember: this is the clipboard and this is where it hangs on the wall. You must be able to find this because this is where you can read the day's schedule. Here you can find out which house you're going to eat that day's meals in and can learn if you're asked to work or study during the morning. Everything else will make sense with time. And, if you really forget, someone will be happy to help you find the clipboard.

Angus is in information technology and came to L'Abri on the recommendation of a friend. He was whisked over to the Currys' house even before he could be given the tour, and there in the Stables he found a group having lunch together and discussing the loss of the experience of community in contemporary society. After 20 years living in the villages of South Asia, Doug is able to see some characteristics of his Canadian culture more clearly than friends who have spent their whole lives in Vancouver. The content and tone of that first lunchtime conversation intrigued Angus and persuaded him to stay. He still remembers the exhilaration of the moment's surprise when he thought, 'These strange people have their finger on the pulse of society'. He was, he said, 'both intellectually and emotionally stimulated'.

Angus had become a Christian as a teenager but his life was highly compartmentalized. 'It was more about moral living than about knowing God,' he told Doug. 'I was one person with my friends at church and a different person altogether with my other friends. The impossibility of living a moral life consistently became increasingly difficult to sustain.' He felt trapped in a religion he could neither live out morally nor defend intelligently. Unable to explain his faith to his cynically anti-religious parents, his frustration came to a head during a humiliating episode when a friend 'pretty much wiped the floor with me intellectually'. Angus decided he had had enough. 'From that time on I didn't consider myself to be a Christian any more.'

Tom came to L'Abri after a disappointing experience as a missionary in western Africa. He had heard about L'Abri from friends, but by the time he arrived he was fiercely sceptical about organized religion and systematic theology. In fact, his concerns had become so deep that he was suspicious of any form of system, even systematic thought. He had lost his usual talkativeness and hesitated to speak in groups of people he didn't know and trust. Even with his background in ministry, Tom didn't want to read the Bible any more or have anyone read it to him. He was no longer sure about the boundary between help and manipulation. He was ashamed to face his church, the church that had sent him out to be a triumphant minister; and (to be frank) the church was equally embarrassed to face his tormented thoughts.

Natalie had come to spend a year of advanced study at Cambridge University. She had always been advanced, in part because her parents had expended such effort in home-schooling her. She had won every award her high school offered. She was talented and beautiful. No one, including Natalie herself, understood why she was depressed. She visited L'Abri one weekend from Cambridge, looking as ever the bright success in the making. However, the door to my office had barely closed for our chat when she began to weep inconsolably.

Instead of Edith, I happened to give the tour when Paul arrived at the door with the broken sign. I remember that we were just outside the big downstairs bathroom when he turned to me in some concern. 'I can sometimes become psychotic if I don't take my medicine,' he told me. I had studied veterinary medicine before going to theological seminary, but I knew very little about this sort of thing. 'Will we recognize it if you become psychotic?' I asked, just as concerned. Paul was sombre. 'Usually I think I'm Jesus Christ,' he answered. 'I think we'll recognize that,' I said with relief.

So many faces, so many stories: each one valuable, but I can't remember all the names. One woman arrived and found me in the library. She was a nurse in an intensive care unit. I don't know how she found out about L'Abri. Almost her first words were a challenge, issued in a soft voice: 'I want you to prove to

me that Jesus rose from the dead.' I asked her a few questions,
and of course the motivation for her request was simple. She
reasoned that if Jesus really rose from the dead and she could
be convinced of it, she would then be able to believe all that he
taught. She hoped that the rest of her lost religious faith would
come flowing back in the wake of a renewed confidence in
the Resurrection. Doubtless she had seen a lot of things at the
hospital where she worked that had caused her to doubt both
the existence of God and the possibility of rising from the dead.

I don't know why I pursued the question in such an odd way,
but I decided to ask her how she knew that anything at all was
true. She replied that she was sure of nothing.

This didn't seem very likely to me, and so I began again:
'Well, take North America, for example. Have you ever been to
North America?'

She shook her head.

'But you know that there is such a place as North America,'
I went on, 'even though you've never been—'

But before I could go any further, she was weeping and
confessing that, strange as it sounded, she was no longer sure
that there was. Just because I claimed to be from there or
because I could show her photographs or envelopes with stamps
from Canada, nothing would be able to make her certain that
such a place really existed. Nurses from intensive care units are
highly trained and intelligent people. They are not fools, and
they know a lot about how the world works. But something in
this woman's story had destroyed her confidence that human
beings can know anything at all. She was damaged, and damaged
in a way that causes a person a huge amount of grief.

It is, I hope everyone will agree, easier to persuade someone
of the reality of North America than of the historicity of Jesus'
resurrection. I was glad she had come to L'Abri. In the years
since her arrival I have spoken with several people just as
confused about how they could be confident about anything. She
was not so unusual after all. It would be a very serious mistake

to disregard her pain as something weird and laughable. Such stories are becoming common.


Fiona, Angus, Tom, Natalie and the ICU nurse—the students at L'Abri come from every country and every religious persuasion. They come for all sorts of reasons. They arrive nervous and not knowing what to expect, but three days later they may be giving the tour of the house quite comfortably to some even newer arrival if Edith is in her kitchen cooking. We see more and more students from the former Soviet Union, and have begun to have Indians arrive with questions about postmodern culture I had assumed were of interest only to Westerners. A German physicist specializing in high-temperature superconductors may find herself on arrival sitting next to a homeless junkie from Scotland. Neither has ever met anyone like the other before. They begin suspiciously, convinced that the other has nothing to teach them, but by the end of the first week they may be good friends. They may help each other to believe that God exists and loves them. These things really do happen. We have seen them occur in our houses.

Everyone approaches this life together with different worries. A recent American student was obviously ill at ease because there seemed to be so few rules governing the place. In the first few days of her visit she asked one or another of us who live here the policy on a host of issues. The subject of boundaries came up in all sorts of contexts. My wife, Chryse, was amused when she asked about the rules concerning shoes and if she would be allowed to go barefoot in the Manor even though it was very cold. Chryse was amused, but she was also wise enough to realize that this woman was incapable of living with any degree of ambiguity. Everything had to be legislated for her if she was to be comfortable with her surroundings.

This is not a recipe for a flourishing life, not because in the end everything is relative or lacks significance but because we must learn to approve or disapprove for ourselves so much that comes to us. The reality created for us by the Living God, though it has a moral nature, is not meant to be universally regulated and prescribed. There are boundaries, but there is freedom within them. Of course, others living and studying with us at L'Abri may chafe at the schedule we have and such rules as there are. One of the dynamic things about learning together is that people with these two opposite intuitions about how life should be can arrive together and share a room for three months.

We have terms at L'Abri, but students can come for as little as an afternoon or as long as three months. It is rare that someone leaves sooner than they planned, but hundreds ask if they can prolong their stay once they get past the awkwardness of their first day or two. I was dismayed, therefore, when Stefan from Denmark left without saying goodbye. He had only just arrived, but I'd heard that he would be with us for several weeks. I had barely met him, and then he left unexpectedly. I feared that we had neglected him in some way, perhaps not welcomed him sufficiently—and, given the importance we attach to each arrival, such a departure could signal a real failure on our part.

My German colleague Rüdiger Sumann, however, laughed at my discomfort, because he had learned Stefan's real story. He had only very recently become a Christian from a background with no religion in it at all, and he was understandably eager to learn more about spiritual truth and all it had to teach him about how to live. He had assumed that he needed to go somewhere far away and unfamiliar and there acquire a great deal of new information. He had his tour of the house and then launched immediately into absorbing lecture materials in our study room. But the very first few things he listened to brought home to him that for many years he had been a very bad son. A better course of action than to spend weeks in a foreign community might be to return to Copenhagen, to find a good local church fellowship and begin explaining and expressing his new faith in Jesus Christ to his family. Rüdiger met with Stefan and after listening to him agreed that it was a good idea for him to leave L'Abri early and follow this new path. The lessons he needed to learn would be best learned very near to home. It was, in this instance, a sudden departure that was itself an encouragement.

The community of L'Abri is not perfect, and I must not leave the wrong impression or only tell tales of obvious success and keep silent about our faithlessness. We are as cracked and faulty as the sign on our front door. I mean this—I am not just saying humble words to win acceptance. We are weak and very poor ambassadors for the Lord God, but he has been generous to us and for 50 years he has continued to send people to stay with us. We do not know how much longer it will all continue.

There have been some changes in the visitors during that time. The rate at which Western culture has shifted is staggering. As a general rule, students stay longer at L'Abri than they used to. This is at least partly because they seem more doubtful that true ideas may help to solve their perceived problems. They also seem to be more distrustful that a person trying to explain to them true ideas is actually hiding some personal agenda. And the questions they arrive with have also changed to a degree. There are fewer questions nowadays about metaphysics, about whether God exists. People are much more likely to concede that God does exist—and even that Christianity is the true account of that God. But, with this concession, they are less likely to accept that his existence alone entitles God to our love or worship or obedience. They suspect that actually they are at least God's moral equivalent, if not his better.

Schaeffer used to speak about the need for people to bow twice before God: once as sinners before a judge and once again as creatures before the Creator. It was after I had given a lecture entitled 'Is God Fair?' that Rüdiger remarked to me that, though these two bows remain unchanged, they have certainly changed places in terms of which is the more difficult and offensive. In the not too distant past, it was the first bow that so offended: to bow as a sinner meant admitting guilt and powerlessness and a need of help and forgiveness. Today, that makes sense to many of us. Very few people nowadays live in the silly denial that they are messed up and damaged, that they need help from some quarter. But the other bow—as a creature before the Creator—is today's sticking-point. It's highly offensive. What made sense to many of our grandparents is now a real obstacle. We have lost the distinction between creature and Creator. We think we have as much right to be at the centre and to determine reality as anyone else—including God. We even feel ourselves capable of judging him.

An example of these changes is provided by the contemporary Brazilian author Paulo Coelho. He has been one of the 10-best-selling authors internationally, and much of this huge popularity is because he so perfectly expresses the 'common-sense popular theology' of our time. In two of his novels (and this shows that this is an important concept to him) he has characters inventing a new ritual for the Day of Atonement. The concept is Jewish, of course: a special day on which people are publicly cleansed and forgiven for the transgressions of the previous year. The Jewish idea is then fulfilled perfectly in the death of the Messiah. Coelho's ritual, however, comprises two parts—in fact, two lists. The first is a list of the people's sins against God, for which they ask forgiveness. The second list the people hold up to the sky is an account of the evils that have occurred to them in the past year, the pains and disappointments for which they hold God responsible: what they regard as God's sins against them. People are forgiven by God and they claim the right in turn to forgive him. This is the equality our generation thinks it has with the Creator. We may be willing to bow before God but we also suspect that God needs to bow before us.

Children ask questions because they want to know the answer. Adults ask questions from many motives. Sometimes a question is a test: are you going to stick with me, or are you going to leave me when I get honest and inconvenient?

Sometimes a question is a barrier used to keep others away from
the real issues in the questioner's heart. Sometimes—and this is
the worst kind—a person asks questions because they are sure
there's no answer and they want to look smart, or they want
to drag others down into the same swamp in which they are
drowning.

But in fact there are fewer questions at all these days, in my
experience. People arrive at L'Abri for many reasons, but more
and more they come knowing only that something is wrong.
They are unhappy and dissatisfied. Nothing really has a taste.
They are full of disappointment and frustration. Affluence or
education or relationships have not yet healed some wound
in their heart. They don't think they have any great interest in
anything as abstract-sounding as a 'worldview'. The Christians
who come may claim to know everything about the gospel as
told in the Bible but they insist that they feel nothing towards
it. The message doesn't produce the emotions they long for.
They doubt that a new idea, even a new truth, can solve their
emotional pain, a pain that can turn into emotional numbness.
More and more students admit to cutting themselves, and one
reason for hurting yourself in this fashion is that some sensation
at least is better than none at all.

These are big challenges to face. We have to listen carefully,
remembering that the same question is different depending on
who is asking it. There are patterns, but there are no 'cases' or
'syndromes'. We are not to offer people a formula that fits our
diagnosis. And yet. And yet. We can take great comfort from
the fact that, however the world changes, and although every
student is an individual, L'Abri has to change very little. When
someone arrives, you should greet them and welcome them into
your home and into your life. This is where it has always begun,
and where, I think, it always will.

# Acting as if God Lives Somewhere Nearby

*"The inward area is the first place of the loss of true spirituality. The outward is always just the result of it."*

Francis Schaeffer

Several years ago, a German friend of mine who is a New Testament scholar was talking to me about a problem I was experiencing. I think it's fascinating that I no longer remember what the problem was but I still think about what he said to me. We were in a sandwich shop, sitting in a booth, the smell of new-baked bread all around us. He held in his hand a letter I had written him, and the page was literally tear-stained. He is a kind man and with a wisdom to match his intelligence. 'You L'Abri people have a basic problem,' he said to me. 'You demand reality all the time.'

It was a very puzzling thing to say. At first blush, there seems to be no acceptable alternative. Do we really want to accept unreality in some aspect of our life? He must have said it to me five or six years ago, and I still ask myself what the words meant and in what sense it was a justifiable criticism. Christian discipleship is about knowing God. This, after all, is what Jesus said: 'Now this is eternal life: that they may know you, the only true God, and Jesus Christ, whom you have sent.'[1] But our generation is quick to reject this notion. We insist that discipleship cannot be merely about knowledge. That

[1] John 17:3

would make it too abstract, and merely a mental construct. If discipleship is about knowledge, it leaves out too much, including some of the most important things about being human. Where, for example, is there room in knowledge for devotion and emotion and relationship and action?

I am sympathetic in many ways to this insistence. Christian discipleship must not be limited to a knowledge that remains small and abstract only. But this is not what we mean at L'Abri when we place so much emphasis on knowing what is true about God, and nor was Jesus speaking of a barren intellectual assent. If my so-called knowledge of the truth does not manifest itself in actions or in obedience to this only true God, you are right to say I don't know him, not really. I know him after a fashion and to a degree, but not really.

And yet all of us sense that knowledge that leads to action is still not sufficient. We can all picture plenty of religious people, full of doctrine and true ideas about God, and we can imagine that these people obey. They are careful not to touch any unclean thing; they refrain from everything that contaminates body or spirit. Nevertheless, we can imagine that these same knowing and obedient people lack joy and gratitude in their discipleship. It is said less often, but I believe it is no less true, that if I lack joy and gratitude I do not know this only true God, not really. I know him after a fashion and to a degree, but not really.

We are used to our sermons ending with a section intended 'for application'. And this is a good thing, because we don't want God's call to us to be restricted to the realm of ideas only. But we are less used to recognizing that if knowledge and obedience do not lead us to joy and gratitude, we have a problem as serious as ignorance and as serious as disobedience. It is no small matter, as I once seemed to think, to say: 'I know the truth and I obey what I know. I just have this small problem of not being grateful to God.'

None of us, however, attain full knowledge, flawless obedience or perfect gratitude. A theology that leads people to expect these will crush us and disappoint us. But does our imperfection in these areas mean that we don't know God, not really? Thankfully, God's generosity and grace cover our imperfections with the righteousness of Jesus Christ, whom he sent. Discipleship is a noun. The New Testament is more likely to use the term 'walking in the Spirit' or some other verb. This walking is an integration of thought and behaviour and emotion, each of them living out our reconciliation with God through his Son. But this also means that Christian discipleship is a long, strange process. Time and again, even after we thought we knew something, we have an experience like scales falling from our eyes and we say, 'Now I see it! Now I know it! Really!'

It is one of my favourite moments at L'Abri—and I'm very glad to say that it doesn't happen that infrequently—when someone runs in, perhaps waving a book or brandishing a tape recorder at me, and says with great conviction, 'Christianity is true!'

'But you would have said that the first day you arrived,' I may respond.

'Yes,' they acknowledge, but as if I am missing the point entirely. 'But I mean it's really true.'

They insist that they're saying something new, and I believe them. The knowledge they already possessed to some degree has grown deeper. This can happen to obedience as well: some duty takes on greater urgency and importance, a person can suddenly see the point behind what was previously a senseless action. It can also happen to joy and gratitude: things long known and obeyed may become a source of new love and appreciation for the only true God.

We are to be integrated in our thought, behaviour and emotion, but we never experience this perfectly. Telling someone that they ought to feel grateful rarely seems to make them so—though it often manages to generate guilt. Learning to seek the perfect agreement between our doctrine and our actions and our feelings is a part of discipleship. However, learning to live while not perfectly integrated is also a part of discipleship. This comes as a welcome revelation to many people.

Dawn Dahl is a L'Abri worker from Iowa who used to live in the top flat of the Manor House, where her life was almost constantly open to observation by the students. She is a source of constant surprise to all of us for many reasons. The most superficial of these is that she loves literature and seems very feminine but she has also driven big green combine harvesters over 'amber waves of grain' and delivered many a lamb on the cold floor of a barn. One day over lunch the discussion revolved around the idea of faith. Ed, a postman from Guildford, not far from the Manor, was present and was obviously seething with anger at much of what he had heard, but he volunteered to do the dishes with Dawn when the meal was over. While they were doing the washing-up together, Ed stepped back from the sink, water dripping from his hands, and asked her if she believed 100 per cent that Christianity was true.

She said she was sure but not 100 per cent. Then he asked her a very personal question: What was she most afraid of? Dawn felt torn between giving an honest answer and being a good example to someone who was having such difficulty believing the Christian message. With a sense that she was being frank but perhaps doing lasting damage, she replied that her greatest fear was that she would wake one day to find that none of what she had believed and taught others to believe was true. Ed began to sob and said that that was the sort of faith he could hope for. What Dawn was describing was an integration of the whole person. She was being honest about her limitations and her fears, and yet she lived with integrity in the tension. He had been able to observe her and had seen it for himself.

Monday is a day of prayer at every branch of L'Abri around the world. We see our colleagues in other countries so infrequently that it's encouraging to know we are all spending the day with a greater emphasis on giving God our thanks and telling him our needs. It's something I think of us as doing together in a spiritual reality. It is the very heart of our life before God and much more crucial for us than the meals and the lectures and the tutoring.

The origin of this day of prayer, as of so many things, lies in the experience of the Schaeffer family. Susan was a young girl. She had been sent by the family to occupy their new chalet before the rest of them could arrive and it was a heavy responsibility. The family was facing real tests of their dependence on God. They lacked even enough money to buy food. Where were they to get it now they had left the safety of their mission organization? While Susan waited in the lonely house, she had some remarkable thoughts, thoughts that showed much greater faith than many of her elders. They must pray diligently, and they should all take part in the labour of prayer. And so, when the family arrived, she suggested that they divide the day into slots and that everyone take turns praying for the things they needed God to give them. They set aside a room for this, and the whole family—and a visitor living with them at the time—prayed in turn throughout the day.

We continue to this day to ask God to send us people—workers as well as students—rather than actively recruiting them. We ask God to provide for us financially, rather than inviting people to support us, even though we know that many would be glad to do so. This kind of 'faith mission' draws on the heritage and influence of others before us, such as George Müller and Hudson Taylor and the China Inland Mission. Although in some ways this real dependence must be the experience of every Christian and every Christian ministry, L'Abri doesn't think it wrong if other organizations advertise for staff or students or fundraise appropriately; but we try to institutionalize our dependence on God, to incorporate it into

our operating principles. When God ceases to provide, our
intention is to close our doors and sell our properties and let
L'Abri die. Although this will be hard and will doubtless test our
resolve, we don't believe that God wants the fellowship of L'Abri
to endure. It is only the Church that lasts and lasts.

We weave this failure-unless-God-shows-up factor into
our life also as part of our proclamation that God is real. It is a
potent argument and very challenging to anyone who doesn't
expect to see prayers answered very specifically over the course
of their stay. After all, our faith is to rest not on human wisdom
but on the power of God.[2] And in a distrustful age, when people
claim to detect a hidden agenda behind everything that purports
to be good, it is wonderful for a student to know that we will
never ask them for money beyond the cost to us of their room
and board. L'Abri is an attempt to offer shelter not from the
realities of a world in bondage to decay but from suspicion and
cynicism and the methods of the worldly-wise.

We also continue to pray for God's guidance, for the Holy
Spirit truly to be with us in our decisions. All of our teaching
insists (because this is what the Bible tells us) that the Creator is
still active and involved in the world and its history. And because
we know this we must move on from this to prayer. He is not a
do-nothing god, a god that remains a concept from which we
take only intellectual comfort.

Of course, our reliance on God brings its difficulties. We
struggle with all the issues of knowing God's guidance (and
much could be said on this). We struggle with the sense of
passivity, some of us more than others. I, as a bad example, am
by nature an activist and to be honest I fail in two ways. First,
I prefer to be doing something, to be seen to do something, to
create a noise. I prefer almost anything to being quiet before
God and expecting him to act on my behalf. I want to exult in
my strengths and abilities, not in my weakness. For me, prayer
is work. I claim to have learned the lesson that God can achieve

[2] 1 Corinthians 2:5

more, and more that is worthwhile, when I wait for him than I can accomplish by all my anxious and frenetic activity. I claim to know this and obey this and be grateful for this, but discipleship often means growing slowly, repeating lessons, relearning things at a deeper level.

The second way I fail is more surprising and hard to relate. I fail frequently when God answers a request for wisdom and the time comes for obedient action. You would expect that someone who prefers to be doing would readily leap to it as soon as the work of prayer is done and they are aware of what God requires. But I find it's not always so. I claim ignorance. I say I don't understand. I remain at prayer even though it has ceased to be work and has become sinful disobedience. This may sound shocking. How can something as precious as prayer be wrong?

I am reminded of a church camp I spoke at in Hungary. I had been asked to be there for a week, slowly developing through a series of talks what Jesus meant when he prayed that his followers should be in the world but not of it. I presented a succession of interconnected ideas about culture and the world. This was an unusual time in Hungary, a country rich in history and talent then reinventing itself and its institutions in the wake of the demise of communism and in anticipation of joining the European Union. So, these people hung upon my words—and yet they were careful thinkers and were not just going to accept the notions of some foreigner, and so they asked me questions about work and about the role Christians should have in their society.

At dinner one evening, two women sat with me. Their faces showed how serious they were. If they accepted what I had been saying and acted on it, they told me, it was going to cost them dearly. The workplace in Hungary is frequently hostile to a Christian conscience.

'Then who is going to change Hungary?' I asked.

And one of them, a young woman but with considerable management responsibilities, replied immediately: 'God will have to do it.'

You would need to have heard the tone of her voice to know her meaning. 'God will have to do it' can be a beautiful thing to say, if by that we are saying, 'This is too large a task for any human strength and wisdom. We need God's help to do the right thing.' In saying 'God will have to do it,' you would be rejecting the notion of a do-nothing god. On the other hand—and one must say this gently—we can declare, 'God will have to do it' and be saying something very ugly. The very same words that might have been so beautiful are ugly and unfaithful if we mean by them 'I know what God requires of me in this situation but I don't trust him enough to obey him. God is going to have to accomplish his will without my co-operation. To obey would be too costly.' In other words, we can hide behind devout language, claiming to believe in God's power when actually we are being do-nothing people. We can continue to pray after it has ceased to be work and has become unfaithfulness.

I find that I fail in both these ways: acting as if God does nothing, leaving prayer as merely an intellectual concept, talking about it—even writing about it in books—without it being the reality in my life; but also staying at prayer too long, asking God to act on my behalf even after I am aware of his will and command. Both sorts of failure display a fundamental distrust of God.

People pay a great deal of attention today to mechanisms and formats, seeking the right style and method of prayer. And this is understandable. In an age that is suspicious of words and their hidden agendas, there is widespread dissatisfaction with any form of prayer that is primarily verbal or logocentric. And in an age that wants to see that things matter, that things other than knowing what the truth is matter, there is dissatisfaction with any form of prayer that is as loud and verbose as our insolent media. We are deeply unhappy with prayer that seems to engage only the mind and not the whole heart and body and being. We long for a sense of transcendence today just as we longed for a sense of God's immanence in the 1960s.

Ours is also an age highly aware of competing techniques of prayer and spiritual disciplines. These different forms come to us from various Christian traditions and from outside Christianity altogether. My colleague Andrew Fellows first pointed this out to me in a lecture on Neopaganism. This is a spirituality that is growing in popularity in England probably for many reasons but not least because it 'maps onto' our present dissatisfaction with evangelical Christianity. Neopaganism is friendly to feminism and to environmental issues, it generally eschews organized religion and doctrine and it has an embodied spirituality that gives its adherents things to do, rituals to observe and rhythms to live by.

We would be very unwise not to listen to the complaints of the people in our churches, even if they are not well defined or expressed. And it would be wrong-headed not to attend to what it is our contemporaries find satisfying in non-Christian practices. But it is equally mistaken to spend all our effort in a search for the right method, something that feels relevant and satisfying. No perfect form is going to prevent prayer from being work. No technique is going to ensure that we rise from prayer when it's time for prayer to end and action to begin. Coming to God in spiritual reality and true dependence can be done in many ways, and it is of crucial importance for people today to see that God listens, cares about our concerns and still acts on the requests made of him by his people. These things carry much greater weight than the proper posture or form or ritual.

God wishes good things for his children, and yet our world is cursed with frustration and in bondage to decay.[3] God still hears and acts, and yet not every prayer is answered. This is the reality

[3] Romans 8:21–22

we live in, and the Bible paints an accurate picture of how we experience it. Martin Luther observed that humankind acts like a drunk trying to climb onto a horse: forever mounting on one side only to fall off the other, again and again. And we can see this sort of reaction and counter-reaction when we consider our experience of prayer.

On the one hand, the church can try to protect God's reputation by removing him from the tangle of real, everyday life. Once in Annapolis, Maryland I was giving a lecture on film. When we came to the questions at the end, a woman sitting in the very front row said, 'It's clear from listening to you that you think the Bible is true. Can you tell me why you think that?' This was completely off the subject but it's a question one never ignores, whatever the occasion. I apologized and said that I would very quickly give some reasons for my confidence in the Bible, but that my answer would probably be very inadequate because a string of assertions is not the same thing as a careful argument. The very last reason I gave was my subjective experience of the way the God of the Bible continued to act and to answer prayer. She seemed satisfied, and the workshop went on with its discussion about film; but after the audience was dismissed a tall figure stayed behind to introduce himself. He was an elder from my own denomination, it turned out, who shared many of my own doctrines and convictions. He told me he appreciated my answer about the Bible, but proceeded to say that he thought it improper for me to end with a reference to my experience of God's activity. His reasoning, I believe, was that this was too subjective and it raised the problem of unanswered prayers.

This is the wrong track to take. It's certainly not the track taken by the Bible. God may or may not act to protect us, for example—as in the case of the three Jewish exiles facing execution in Babylon for not engaging in false worship. We can't be sure how God is going to respond in a given situation, but he certainly doesn't need our protection. We find his poets frequently complaining in their psalms, in terms of the utmost distress, about God's apparent distance and lack of involvement in their lives. They could only complain in this way because their expectations were otherwise. My colleague Andrew has also shown me how important it is for the church, as a people awaiting a city not yet seen, to be free to lament before God as the Jews were free to lament. The groaning of God's people has not ended with the first coming of the Messiah. It only ceases when the Kingdom arrives in its fullness and finality.

This, then, is one side of the horse: praying without expectation of satisfaction. The church, however, often falls off on the other side. We don't want to protect God from the mess of mundane existence and so we interpret all our experience in cosmic, super-spiritual terms. Rather than denying that we are right to hope for God's deliverance in our daily circumstances, we try to see God's action clearly in every situation. On this side of the horse, everything becomes gigantically subjective. When a friend tells me that God once filled up the tank of his car, I have to admit that I'm dubious. God could do it—I believe that he can act and does act, and that is the reality we must live in. But if I express my incredulity to my friend, he takes it as a slight on God's character and thinks me unspiritual and faithless.

I was driving once to a Sunday evening fellowship group in the hills around Austin, Texas and was listening to the radio on the way. National Public Radio was reporting on a severe drought in Florida which was badly affecting farmers. Later that evening, as our group shared the things we wanted to pray about, a young woman asked us to pray that it wouldn't rain on the weekend of her wedding because she was planning an outdoor reception. And, as you can guess, the wedding was to be later that month in Florida.

On this side of Luther's horse, if any prayer goes unanswered, or if there is any resolution that doesn't fulfil my own personal desire, it may lead me to the conclusion that the problem is something in me: my sin, my lack of faith. On this side of the horse it isn't easily conceded that bad things continue to happen—even to God's children—in a cursed and frustrated world in bondage to decay. Orchards do die for want of rain, and some of them are owned by Christians. Wedding receptions do get washed out, even if the couple have prayed about it. The focus of my attention on this side of the horse is on maintaining my confidence that God will answer my prayer, but I may think that I have to be, and remain, completely free of doubt. I must be able to insist that I know how God is going to respond to my circumstances—indeed, it is this confident insistence that is required if God is to act. I demand satisfaction and pretend always to experience it.

Neither side of this particular issue is the truth. We must sober up and sit on the horse squarely. The difficulties we encounter must not keep us from honest prayer about our anxieties. I know what my desires are and I make my requests to God as I have been instructed to do; but I don't pretend to know infallibly what God is going to do about them. The point of the parable of the mustard seed is not that we must pay attention to the seed: we realize that the seed is tiny, and our focus is rather on how large the God is on whom we attend. However, neither do we try to hide God behind our doctrine of his sovereignty. It is this very sovereignty that makes us able to go to him in reality, accepting that our desires may be disappointed or fulfilled. We trust him more than we trust ourselves.

And here, I suppose, is what my friend the New Testament scholar may have been hinting at. I have observed that fears often come in pairs. Very frequently I have seen people backing away from one threat, the one in front of them, one they are very aware of—perhaps even too aware of—and all the time they are backing towards another threat, one behind them, one they fear less but are actually much more likely to succumb to. We see this dynamic often in our doctrines. For example, evangelical Protestants may be so afraid of the false doctrine of 'salvation by works' that they keep their eyes fixed on it. They are terrified of falling into that pit even though they are in very little danger of doing so. In the meantime, they are all the while backing into making the gospel something that is only in the mind, a system of belief that merely requires intellectual assent and makes no demands for effort or action. The gospel that remains only an idea in my mind is just as unbiblical as salvation by works, but we so often fear the thing that presents the lesser threat to us.

In this way, as we insist on reality in our walk before God and our prayers to him, we can have too high an expectation of ourselves. We may be demanding experiences that God does not intend us to have. We may so fear a lack of reality in what we tend to call our 'religious' life that we can walk backwards into losing the reality of the spiritual in our everyday, mundane existence. This expectation of a profound religious experience at the cost of a daily reality is what Schaeffer termed 'hyper-spirituality'. Perhaps if we expect everything in our lives to become sacred, to be worship, we can lose the capacity to flourish in obscurity, because we demand that everything should be dramatic and noteworthy. We want our everyday existence in God's world to be fit material for a book.

I will try to tell a story briefly about these things. My wife and I had met Ranald and Susan Macaulay, who founded the English branch of L'Abri, when they came to speak at a conference in Nepal. I was so intrigued by what they said that I got myself appointed their guide in Kathmandu and bounced around with them in the back of a Land Rover for a couple of days seeing the sights. The conversations we had led to a correspondence that resulted in me going to theological seminary. I studied with the hope of working in this strange community I had heard about and read about but had never seen.

So, after years of preparation, Chryse and I came to L'Abri, and we found it more, not less, than we had hoped it might be. There was a reality in what these people were attempting to do together. My years of studying art and then studying science had previously suggested a lack of focus, but at L'Abri my diverse background became useful as I spoke with people fluent in these different 'dialects'. I mention this background only to give you an idea of the depth of our gratitude and satisfaction. Much that had not made sense in our experience now appeared to be full of plan and purpose and providence. We enjoyed the work at the Manor, even though being constantly with other people was exhausting. We felt made for this life.

Imagine our confusion, therefore, when the British Home Office refused us visas and told us to leave the country. They wondered why American citizens, rather than Europeans, were needed to staff this 'study centre'.

Ours was a test case, and it was important for L'Abri to persuade the Government that it is a missionary organization and can therefore employ foreign nationals. So of course we began praying, telling God of our desires and asking him to work on our behalf in the mazes of the British Civil Service. We dared to ask him for ludicrously practical help. We needed a solicitor to represent us, and it would be best if this person was experienced in the intricacies of immigration law; but because L'Abri is so difficult to understand it would be ideal if our solicitor also knew something about our strange fellowship. And, since this was a wholly unforeseen expense, we asked whether it would be possible for this solicitor to represent us without charging us any fee.

I believe it is accurate—though I wasn't keeping a diary—that it was the day after we prayed this that I received a phone call. I remember standing in the long hall of the Pump House and hearing a woman's voice go through the litany, as if she had been listening to our request. She had heard about us and our situation through a friend. She was a solicitor who specialized in immigration law and she considered our case important because she had once studied at L'Abri. Would we be interested in her handling the matter if she waived the usual fees?

Such a rapid and complete answer to prayer was remarkable. It seemed to promise that everything was going to be all right, that we had no cause for alarm. This early hopefulness therefore made the ensuing confusion only that much deeper. The Home Office refused the appeals made on our behalf—though we could continue to live in England and work at L'Abri while the process ground slowly on. The uncertainty weighed very heavily on us as a family and as a fellowship. Setbacks in the case continued. Finally, Chryse and I found ourselves seemingly exiled to America without any plans or any notion of what to do while we waited the years it might take for the matter finally to be settled.

Where was God in this? Why would he grant our wishes to serve him in such a fitting way only to take it from us? Why would he have so clearly answered a prayer and then frustrated us so completely? Was this in response to some personal failing on our part (and I could think of many)? I wish I could honestly report that I was full of confidence in God during this time— not that I was certain that we would return to England and L'Abri but that I trusted that, whatever transpired, he was with us and cared for us. The facts, however, are otherwise. I felt that my life in some senses was over and, as one author has put it, 'so flat that I could see the gravestone at the end'. I was angry— and this even though many things were happening that were marvellous. We were given the use of a flat and a car in St Louis that belonged to the people who were living in our house and using our car in England. I began studies that my years at L'Abri had showed that I needed. I found a very useful job at Covenant Seminary. There were many, many proofs that, far from being forgotten, we were being tenderly cared for; but I had very dim vision and could not see it.

And then, after four years of waiting, our case actually arrived before a magistrate instead of the faceless bureaucrats, and it took only moments to resolve it and we were free to return.

Life is complex. It is never as neat as a Hollywood screenplay. Not everything is clear even in hindsight. If things always

[4] 1 Peter 1:3–9

resolved themselves justly, there would be no need to await
the final judgement of the Creator on the story. Every evil
or disappointment that comes our way is not in reality some
hidden good, intended to teach us and fulfil us—though it can
be used to refine our faith like gold.[4] But on this one episode
in our experience, more full of fears and disappointments and
embarrassments than I have recounted here, I can look back
with gratitude. On our return to England we were happy, but
it took several years and the slow turn of further events before
I could see that the time in America had also been needed.
We had been exquisitely prepared for new opportunities to
serve God in England, and these could not have arisen had we
remained comfortably employed at the Manor.

I am like a drunk trying to ride on a horse. As I look back, I
do see that the horse and I have made progress along the road.
It would be wonderful if I could stay in the saddle a little longer
between falls.

# Talking with Your Mouth Full Can Be a Thing of Beauty

*"We all tend to emphasize big works and big places, but all such emphasis is of the flesh."*
Francis Schaeffer

Long before I ever imagined that I would live and work at L'Abri I was a veterinary missionary in the hills of Nepal. During the visit of Ranald and Susan Macaulay to that country, I had heard about this study centre that had teaching materials on so many subjects. I wrote and asked them to send me the three tapes on Buddhism. These were by a former Zen monk, and I was keenly interested because I was meeting more and more Sherpas in my work and their religion is in the family of Buddhism. While I was about it, I also asked for the two tapes on Hinduism, because all my neighbours were Hindus.

The tapes on Buddhism were helpful but mostly routine in their presentation, but those on Hinduism seemed at first bizarre. It was a rather rambling discussion, and there was all this distracting background noise. There was murmuring and clinking, and it took me some time to realize that the conversation was being taped around a table and that everyone involved in it was eating. The ideas being debated were bracing, but the voice of the man who was leading the discussion was high and a little irritating—especially when he got passionate—and he was very capable of pronouncing the same word two different ways in the space of a few minutes.

This was almost my introduction to Francis Schaeffer. At
university I had seen portions of a film made by him, and again
the ideas were bracing but the fellow wore strange clothes
and made an odd impression on me. I have heard it said that
he never intended his conversations over lunch, or even his
lectures, to be recorded, as he much preferred speaking in real
time and face-to-face with people who came to visit. However, a
student who thought that too much good teaching was going to
waste (and who also ended up working in L'Abri) took to hiding
a microphone in the flowers on the table without Schaeffer's
knowledge. I think the story is probably true. The sound quality
on a lot of the early material certainly suggests it now.

We spend a lot of time at L'Abri around tables together, and
most lunchtimes are referred to as 'formal'. I remember my first
formal lunch as a student. I was so eager to be there. By this
time I had gone to theological seminary, where I had chosen my
coursework according to what I imagined would be useful in a
setting such as L'Abri, and after the years of earnest preparation
I wanted to make a great impression. Everyone assigned to eat
with the MacGregor family had found their way to the back
flat of the Manor and found a chair around the long wooden
table. But I hadn't quite caught the concept. I began introducing
myself around and engaging my neighbours to either side and
across from me in keen conversation. I was so enthusiastic
then that I would not be surprised to be told that I was trying
to juggle three conversations at once. Jock sat at the head of
the table and, after we were all served our food, he caught my
attention and said, with great gentleness, 'At a formal lunch we
try to have one conversation, all of us together.'

I was mortified—but Jock wasn't being authoritarian, he was
merely committed to including everyone in the conversation.
The topic could be anything. There was no approved or
forbidden list of subjects. We needed to listen to each other,
however, even if we found the opinion being expressed offensive.

We spend a lot of time in these discussions, and that of course means that a lot of time is spent in preparing food. The kitchens of the family homes are seldom quiet: there is always another meal to make. But they are not like the kitchens of your favourite Italian or Indian restaurant—places whose products you enjoy but you would rather not see what goes on there. The kitchens at L'Abri are another place where conversations take place amid the dicing and grating. A meal is seen as an event, an event worth thinking about and making beautiful. And we consider the preparation an event also: a combination of the domestic, mundane, everyday and the possibility of simple, inexpensive elegance. There is something very human about sharing the act of eating together, and it transcends all cultures. The Lord Jesus left us with a meal to commemorate his death until his return, when we will join the wedding feast prepared for us.

This attitude is novel and strange to a growing number of our students. We have all heard how it is increasingly rare today for people to sit down and eat together, as families or otherwise. I have an acquaintance who admitted that in the three months since he had moved into his new flat in Bristol he had yet to cook a meal at home. But this is another one of Luther's horses, because when we begin to think of hospitality we can make the paralysing mistake of thinking that this means 'entertaining' and putting on a special show at great effort. In England I have read reports of how frightened people are to invite friends from work over for dinner, fearing that what they serve will not be judged good enough. And so people are buying more and more ready-prepared and packaged food but serving it in such a way as to leave the impression they made it themselves. We have people coming to visit us who have never peeled an onion in their lives. Two hours in the kitchen with a worker, growing in understanding of where food comes from and how it is prepared, can be as life-changing these days, and (if I may say so) as spiritual, as a two-hour tutorial on New Testament background studies in first-century Palestine.

The trick of real hospitality is not always to make a special time of the meal but to include people in it naturally. We should include others in what we do and drop entirely the effort to impress them. There is a place for the big feast (and we do have fun celebrating sometimes), but a bowlful of hearty soup and a thick piece of freshly baked bread on a drizzly day can be better than haute cuisine if they come with hospitality as warm as the food: a sense of comfort and welcome, and the wonder of simple pleasure.

Making a meal an event and yet enjoying its preparation are a feat that requires flexibility. Dawn told me a story once that is not unusual. It was the last but one day of term and she was beginning to look forward to a break from constant hospitality. However, this also meant that people were trying to have conversations they might have been putting off for weeks. Dawn was preparing her last formal meal of the term and she had planned a very nice and fairly complicated menu, with lasagne as the main course. She was cooking that morning with a student from the Netherlands, and for some reason her helper chose that moment to ask a question that was very important to her. Dawn kept working away at the cooking as they talked, but in order to give this woman and her question the attention they deserved she admitted to me that her menu changed about every 15 minutes, growing ever more simple as time went on. By the time the other students arrived in her apartment for lunch, they had chilli served to them and very little else.

These mealtimes have changed even over the past 12 years that I have been watching and eating at L'Abri. There are more vegetarians today than there used to be and more people with special dietary needs, and we see more and more students— men as well as women—for whom food is a problem. Perhaps they suffer from anorexia or bulimia. How does one extend hospitality in all this diversity? It is difficult. Everyone has to learn how to co-operate with one another.

The real changes, however, are best observed in the dynamics of the discussions. If people have grown less aware of how to conduct themselves at a sit-down meal with others in a home, they are definitely less used to having an extended conversation on a single topic which includes many individuals and maybe decidedly different opinions. It takes people time to learn how this is done. It doesn't come naturally to many of us today. Once, a pastor from San Diego had spent time with us and I asked him what he had learned during his stay. I am not sure what I expected, but certainly not the answer he gave me. He told me he had 'recovered the lost art of conversation'. Was I disappointed by his response? Maybe a bit at first, but then I began to think how far-reaching that discovery might be in his life and his ministry. Pastors need to learn to listen as well as speak, especially in an age such as ours that is suspicious of any monologue. Often our media give us a monologue, in effect, and we tolerate it, but we appear also to have an insatiable appetite for more talk radio and shows in which the audience gets to speak. The sermon from the pulpit remains a means of grace, but it is viewed with scepticism today as a form of communication. Many people assume that it's a form of oppression, a kind of brainwashing.

So, we can talk about anything. Sometimes it is sublime, but sometimes it is ridiculously homespun. It is wrong to insist that things must always be profound (because life is a very grave thing), but it's equally wrong for us always to remain blithely superficial, refusing to reveal what we think is true.

There are two different ways to decide whether a conversation at the table has been a success, and they don't always agree. By one criterion, it is a success if someone poses a question and it is answered biblically, progress is made, people learn new things, persuasion occurs. By the other criterion, it's a success if everyone participates, everyone's opinion is heard and respected and we all learn what each other thinks and feels. I believe that both criteria are applied at L'Abri.

Most discussions are not memorable, but sometimes they are for an individual. If you remember the ICU nurse I mentioned in the first chapter, you will recall that she had a severe problem with epistemology—that is, how it is that anyone can know anything. At one conversation over lunch we were discussing certainty and epistemology and religious faith. It happened to be raining. I could see this, but the students were all facing me and had their backs to the window. I said simply, by way of an example, 'It's raining outside' and I went on unaware that this simple sentence in the context of that moment and all that followed had changed a woman's life. She told me months later that she had long been plagued by the question of what level of certainty was possible for us in this life. I can remember noticing a strange expression on her face at the other end of that table. That sentence and that discussion made a lasting impression.

Most discussions are not memorable, but sometimes they are for everyone taking part. One summer's day we talked about humour. This may not sound like a fertile topic for a Christian study centre, but we all love humour, love different aspects of it—and yet religious people often don't know how to let their sense of humour sit beside their theology. It was a magical conversation and everyone knew it. It was a success by both criteria. We all glowed after we'd finished. We all remembered it very fondly. At least two years later, I was at a conference in America and someone there who I didn't know and who didn't know me referred to that very conversation at my table in England. They had no idea I was present. That discussion and its reputation had crossed the Atlantic.

But I made a predictable mistake. I tried to repeat that conversation on humour at a different lunch when things were starting slowly, as they sometimes do. After all, I had been present at that earlier, world-famous discussion. I'd hosted it. I thought I could step into the same river again at a different moment and with a different group of people. It was like serving prepackaged food as if it was something I had made myself. Of course it didn't work, and now I'm glad that it didn't, though at the time I was disappointed. Nothing false or destructive was said. No harm was done. Lunches do revisit the same questions time and again, and one says the same things over and over in response; but we cannot return to a place that is gone.

It is, as you can imagine, sometimes a challenge to lead a discussion so that it succeeds by the criterion either of persuasion or of involvement, to lead it and yet maintain a light touch. Although the L'Abri workers who host the meal are themselves persuaded that Christianity is the true story, they have to ensure that there is space at the table for people who are ardent in their disbelief of the Bible and its message. Non-Christian visitors mustn't feel as if they're at an evangelical feeding frenzy and they are tuna amongst sharks. This may at times mean that the workers have to slow down a hasty Christian conclusion offered by an equally ardent student who is confident of what the Bible has to say.

My colleague Andrew admitted to me that he made a mistake once that was only funny now because it had turned out so well—even if it was at the expense of his dignity and reputation. It was Saturday and there was a lunch in the large dining room of the Manor. Twelve or 15 people sat round the table. One of them was a surfer from Oregon who had dropped out of university and had been living with us for some time. Unwilling to call himself a Christian, he seemed to be making slow progress in his studies and Andrew was as protective of him as of a tender plant just breaking through stubborn soil. Also at the table was an Oxford-trained barrister. This fellow had recently stumbled on a book by Schaeffer and it is not an overstatement to say he had been transformed by reading it. It was more than he could have hoped that his faith could be integrated into

everything that he thought and felt and did. Now, his faith was
rational and could welcome argument without hesitation, so
when he learned that L'Abri still existed and there was a branch
nearby, he came down from London to visit us for a weekend in
great enthusiasm.

Andrew wanted to shield the surfer's quiet progress from
the bull-in-a-china-shop confidence of the barrister. He steered
the conversation as best he could, but the barrister soon spotted
the surfer as a target and he kept up a constant pressure on him.
Andrew felt badly, but he had to get up from the table to help
with the washing-up. When it was done, he returned to the
room and wasn't surprised to see the surfer and the barrister still
sitting at the table together. People can be bullied by new arrivals
to L'Abri who have not yet learned how to be patient with others.
What did surprise Andrew a great deal, though, was when the
surfer turned his bushy blond head and announced that he'd
just become a Christian. The ensuing weeks proved that that
moment of conversion was authentic.

It is appreciably harder today than it was even 10 years ago
to have a discussion over lunch that succeeds by either criterion.
People who doubt that new ideas can do anything to salve their
wounds are also less likely to engage in conversations they
regard as abstract and intellectual. The question 'So, what shall
we talk about today?' in the past was often enough to launch us
into the current, but now it can be followed by 20 minutes of
embarrassed silence as people look at their plates and are careful
not to catch my eye. I have let it go that long before. Usually
someone pitches in with a desultory question after a time,
largely to save my face and spare my feelings as the host.

But then I may come upon this very same group engaged
in animated discussion out on the lawn or late at night in the
library. This puzzles me, and I don't think I've yet got to the
bottom of it. At first I was sure that the source of the problem
couldn't be me, for after all I am the moderator of world-famous
conversations. But then I began to fear that I *am* the problem,

perhaps because my beard has now turned white and I look
to young adults like an authority figure, whereas once I didn't.
Recent discussions have brought to light a deep cynicism and
distrust of authority. (American students may have been a brief
exception to this in the aftermath of the attack on the World
Trade Center, but the Europeans only grew more sceptical
as they watched the American reaction.) Or perhaps I'm the
problem because I've become too opinionated, intolerant or
just plain quick to talk, and so the students have learned that
it's easier just to let me waffle on breathlessly—they can have a
really good chat later, on the lawn by themselves. But though my
beard is white and I may tend to talk too much, I have spoken
to colleagues at L'Abri, and not only at my branch, and most of
them admitted that they too were finding it harder to stimulate
interest in lunchtime conversations.

We try to view this as our problem rather than blaming it
on our students. This is not an inconsequential point. If people
today no longer seem to understand language that is precious
to us, or can no longer participate in forms of interaction that
we love and associate with a golden past, we should be like the
Living God and think incarnationally. Human beings who are
hopelessly alienated from the Creator have a serious and deadly
problem, but God chose to view this problem as his own and
made reconciliation possible through the Incarnation. God
came to us as Emmanuel; we did not seek him out. In the same
way, if people today can't comprehend the Bible's message, I
can't change the message but I can view the problem as mine. I
must see that the responsibility for meaningful discourse is my
burden. If they are not interested in the issues I think they ought
to be, I must do the hard work of discovering what does concern
them. Because God is Master of every area of human existence,
the gospel can be applied to everything they are interested in. It's
an act of great love to attempt to communicate with someone
who appears to refuse the invitation. It was in this manner that

the Christ came and dwelt among us, but the people did not receive him.

We considered discontinuing the practice of formal lunches—something that many of our friends consider an essential part of L'Abri's style. As I have said above with regard to prayer, we should listen to the people around us rather than clinging on to treasured cultural expressions. But similarly we must not be obsessed with perfecting techniques. As with prayer, reality can be fostered via different forms. However, the combination of conversation and food—like hospitality—is an element in almost every culture,[5] and this combination should not be abandoned but cultivated. People are less likely to give themselves away or to reveal their inner, cherished thoughts in front of an authority figure they don't yet trust. We therefore have to prove ourselves trustworthy; and this is, of course, by its very nature a process that requires time and patience.

I once asked a Korean pastor at a lunch what he found culturally strange about what we were doing. He startled us all by pointing at Charles, an English student on the other side of the table. Charles was only 15—we rarely accept anyone this young, but we had made an exception for him. He looked fairly 'alternative' and he spent almost all his waking hours listening to jungle music (a form of techno with a rhythm faster than 90 beats a minute). The pastor said, 'To start with, that boy would not speak in my presence. He would listen to me respectfully.' Korean society is beautiful in its respect for one's elders. But I had to reply, 'Yes, at this table Charles can speak as much as you, and everyone has to be respected.'

Reluctance to speak at lunch, however, is not a matter only of distrust of authority or fear of committing oneself publicly and so opening oneself to criticism. Again (and we shall return to this theme over and over again like a leitmotif) it is much more

---

[5] It's true that in Nepal there was never any conversation during a meal but only before it or afterwards, but nonetheless the two did seem to go together.

to do with distrust of things remaining mental constructs not acted on. Conversations that I wouldn't characterize as 'abstract' or 'intellectual' oftentimes are called this by our students—and for them these descriptions are synonymous with 'irrelevant' or 'boring'. Tell me a personal story. Let me tell you how I feel. These things are not boring. These things can't be judged by an authority. These things matter in the real world.

L'Abri has been in existence for half a century and one thing this means is that sometimes we have people come to study with us whose parents had an important experience themselves at a branch long ago. The children's questions, however, are not precisely the same as those of their parents. When a parent comes to visit, they may find the changes in the dynamics around the lunch table confusing, and this tends to make them suspicious that L'Abri has lost its way, pandering to the emotional and psychological at the price of ignoring objective reality and propositional truth.

A father from New Jersey who had a valuable time at L'Abri in the early 1970s was visiting his son who was staying with us in the 21st century. They sat uncomfortably next to one another at the table in my house, near the end of a long, three-month term. I was not looking forward to the next hour and a half because as I looked round the table I saw that those eating with me were the individuals least likely to participate in a formal conversation. This was not going to be a good lunchtime.

A couple of days before this, I had given a lecture on the life of John the Baptist, and since John's example is a source of hope to me I had begun the evening with a brief discussion with the students about heroes and what they expected from the example of others. This had not gone far because, though the audience was cynically relaxed with the concept of 'celebrity', they were very hesitant to name any public figure as a potential hero. They were, in fact, clearly profoundly uncomfortable with the idea. At the lunch, someone wanted to revisit the idea of heroism, and why the discussion had gone so badly (from my middle-aged perspective). I was not thrilled with the suggestion. I wanted the time to go well: I felt the need to prove to the father that things still 'cooked' at L'Abri, that we had retained our touch and our importance.

But what transpired was remarkable and taught me some significant lessons. I very rarely require people to speak or call on them by name, and yet the normally quiet student who suggested we revisit this non-starter of a topic asked everyone around the table to name their hero. People co-operated in a way I don't believe they would have done had I made the suggestion. The people they named were not public figures; they were not names known around the table. They were very private people— frequently parents, or someone doing a small job very faithfully: someone whose constancy meant a great deal to someone sitting at my table but who was otherwise hardly newsworthy. It was a very tender, very surprising conversation. Students who had spoken rarely, and never with a commitment to what they were saying, spoke that afternoon with great passion. People who never showed obvious signs of interest were weeping about their relationship with their hero and their admiration for them in a world in which they trusted and admired few things.

I felt that the conversation was a success by both of our criteria—and so I was dismayed to learn later that the visiting father strongly disapproved of the discussion and the fact that I had allowed it to become so intimate and emotional. The students, however, spoke with great appreciation of that lunch, and as I reflect on it I consider these diverse reactions to be an indication of how differently we view personal relevance. A father may think it appropriate for us to deal with concepts and abstractions but reckon that the personal application should remain private, something to be done as homework rather than in front of an audience. His son, on the other hand, may insist that an issue must plainly be relevant to the individual and that only after we have proved it to be so might it be valuable to consider it as a broader and more abstract principle.

The other day we had a lunchtime discussion at my house that began with the question 'What makes for a good lunch discussion?' We reviewed the criteria and then cited our recent favourites. I was interested to hear that my colleague Rüdiger had come to the table with two questions himself. He asked, 'How do you show love? And how do you like to receive love?' The students enjoyed themselves, and everyone contributed. It was an abstract topic in one way, but in another it was something everyone was involved in. Everyone had an opinion about it, everyone felt it very deeply, and because of this universal and emotional engagement it seemed relevant to them. And surely the gospel is not far removed from the showing and receiving of love.

It is a cliché that 'the only stupid question is one that is left unasked.' It isn't really the case, though. There are other stupid questions, but a better word for them is 'foolish'. One of the most foolish is a question that is not really a question at all. It is asked as if the person posing it wants to learn, and they inflect their voice so that it is understood to be a question, but in reality it is only a pretext for this person to show off their knowledge and drop names they have found in books, in an attempt to get attention or to put other people down. This kind of foolishness is akin to debate. Real debate is a sport not unlike wrestling. Both wrestling and debating are about defeating an opponent. They are both very competitive, and I enjoy them both. In a debate you are not trying to be fair in your argument, you're just trying to impress an audience or a panel of judges. You are not concerned about the truth of your case, and if there is some weakness in your argument your only worry is 'Is my opponent, or are the judges, quick-witted enough to spot it?'

This is not how truth operates, and this is one reason why when I became a Christian I had to drop out of my high school's debating team. Debating is a fine sport and very good at developing certain skills, but I was very sensitive at the time and had a tender conscience. I didn't want to win an argument unless what I was saying was true. If my opponent said something that was right, I wanted to acknowledge it. Christian apologetics and L'Abri lunches should be that way, too.

We are told that the apostles demolished arguments, but this was not mere debate—we are told they demolished 'every pretension that sets itself up against the knowledge of God'.[6] Surely, in a world such as ours, anything that comes between us and knowledge of the Living God is something that deserves to be demolished?

Every opinion around the table can be expressed. We are not interested in debate. If these are the ground rules, it sounds as if a lunchtime discussion at L'Abri must end up with that sort of demand for equal airtime and bland acceptance that characterizes so much public discourse today. The BBC does this by always finding people to represent both sides of an argument, giving them equal say and then moving quickly on to the next subject. Very recently I was invited to give a lecture on a contemporary novelist at a big bookshop in London. They were told I was a Christian and when eventually this registered with them they rang to cancel my appearance. The manager said that if he let me speak he would be obliged to solicit the opinion of a representative of every conceivable religion in his part of London—and that would be an awesome task indeed! This sounds fair-minded, and I understand his plight. But in reality his decision had shut down all public religious discourse in his shop. I had actually been looking forward to being disagreed with. Let any religious opinion that wishes to be heard have its say! The store didn't need to adjudicate and ensure equal airtime. People could understand that the store was not a Christian institution.

Similarly at a lunch we want to encourage conversation but the basis of our mutual respect is not a relativistic belief that

[6] 2 Corinthians 10:5

truth cannot be known or that all opinions are of equal value. All people are of equal value, but many, many opinions simply do not meet the demands of reality. So, it is possible (though we are beginning to lose this possibility to our own detriment, like the bookshop) to tolerate other people while still demolishing ideas that are pretensions set between us and knowing God.

We are discussing things that matter, and therefore it is right that these things should be emotional. Our intellect and our emotions and our behaviour are to be integrated. This of course means that we can hurt one another in conversation. Demolition is a powerful business, and it must be used with extreme care. I find myself very hesitant to bring things of great value to me out into the open where they may be belittled by others, or may even be trampled on.

Andrew told me about a recent conversation in which a European student was incredulous at some of his convictions about sexual morality. 'You've got to be kidding!' he insisted. Modesty and chastity sounded like tunes from a quaint bygone era. However, the diversity of L'Abri then showed its value. An Indian student very quietly told the story of how he had met his wife for the first time at their wedding. Without being crude or explicit, and yet with a powerful intimacy, he described the experience of getting undressed in front of someone you had previously seen only veiled. Every mouth at the table was open in astonishment. What had perhaps sounded primitive and illiberal from Andrew now was revealed as a beautiful and very credible way to find immense satisfaction.

These are moments that one could not possibly plan or orchestrate.

# Beggars Living in the Cathedral

*"If God's people seem to be beaten in a specific battle, not because of sin or lack of commitment or lack of prayer or lack of paying a price but because they have waited on God and refused to resort to the flesh, then they have won."*

Francis Schaeffer

The principle at L'Abri is that we work half the day and study half the day. It is an old rhythm in Christendom.

Everyone is not studying the same thing at L'Abri. There isn't a curriculum that everyone does. People come with different questions pressing upon them. They also come with different knowledge already acquired and different experience accumulated. Nothing is more draining or discouraging than having to fit into a system that pays no attention to your individual curiosity or refuses to recognize where you have already been. In my experience, such systems are usually for the benefit of the teachers rather than the students. However, this should not be a point of pride. Sometimes students don't see that there is wisdom in following a curriculum. You do need calculus before you can do higher physics, and you may need algebra prior to calculus, and you have to be able to multiply before you can do any of them. All students know is that they want to build a warp engine like the one in the film, make the calculations for the jump into hyperspace and whizz over to the desert planet of Tatooine.

I remember a conversation one afternoon in the big Victorian kitchen of the Manor. Autumn sunlight came through the window and made the dust motes dance. I was moaning over our apathy about understanding the world and I gave a pseudo-statistic I had heard somewhere. I mentioned that some very high percentage of American high school graduates was reported to be unable to find their country on an unmarked globe. I was astonished when a British student took me to task over my complaint. 'Of what real use is it to be able to find America on a globe—even for Americans?' he asked. 'Most high school graduates are never going to pilot the space shuttle, so they're not going to have to find anything on a globe. We never see the world as a globe. What is the value of such useless, irrelevant knowledge?' And he wanted to know why I should try to shame people into a sense of inadequacy because of their inability to perform a pointless task.

I was surprised by this response because I thought it was obvious that this statistic was proof of some real failure on the part of our culture. I was also surprised because the man taking me to task was a British primary school teacher, someone I thought would be my ally in observing a crisis in education. But people now distrust the assumption that knowledge is simply valuable in its own right, and they rebel against an authority that preaches this assumption at them. This is one facet of our postmodern day.

Probably half the visitors coming to L'Abri have a notion of what they want to study while with us. Perhaps they've been disturbed by the content of their university studies and so they want to thrash out a Christian perspective on the influence of Nietzsche or Foucault in the social sciences. Maybe it is some doctrine from their childhood that no longer seems obviously true to them as adults—for example, how can we be significant creatures if we live in a universe overseen completely by a sovereign God's providence? Or they may face a particular situation and wish to understand how God communicates his will—they are saying something like, 'I would love to obey God and do whatever he wants, if only I could discover what that is.'

Of those who arrive with something specific they want
to study, half of them discover while with us that there's an
even deeper and more pressing question in their lives than
the familiar one they brought with them. Often they will have
struggled with the issue they're addressing for a long time
without making any progress, and they hope that by coming to
a study centre and devoting time to it they can break out of the
rut they have dug in trying to find an answer. The job of a L'Abri
tutor (and everyone is assigned a tutor to help them make good
use of their studies) is to recognize such patterns and ruts. A
tutor can also help a student to see that they need to answer the
deeper question if they want to go forward.

The rest of the students arrive unsure what they wish to
study, but it doesn't ordinarily remain that way. Usually, the
conversations around the lunch tables or the lectures they
hear suggest subjects they want to understand better. Some
people—in fact, more and more of those who find their way to
the door with the broken sign—have lost their sense of curiosity.
In those who arrive without a question it is often a symptom
of someone who sees no point in learning. They doubt that any
idea can make a real change in their situation, in their emotional
pain, in their distrust and their intuition of meaninglessness. The
British primary school teacher was one of these. The very person
who was meant to awaken children to the marvel of learning
about the created world around them had lost the motivation to
continue learning himself.

My friend Frank Stootman directs the work of L'Abri in
Australia. We got him to come and teach in England once. I
knew that Frank was a scientist and involved in astronomy but
no more than that. One evening during the week of his lectures
we showed the film *Contact*, which tells a tale about Seti—the
search for extra-terrestrial intelligence. In the film—of course—
the Americans discover a signal that hints at alien intelligence,
and they contact colleagues in Australia to try to verify it. Frank
leaned over to me and said, 'That's supposed to be me.' I laughed,

thinking it was a joke, but afterwards I asked him what he had meant and he told me he was chair of Seti in Australia. I was fascinated as he elaborated. He told me he was the only one active on the committee who he knew to be a Christian, but (even more interesting) he said he was the only one who didn't expect Seti to find anything. My two questions were the obvious ones. 'Then why did they make you the chairman?' I asked first. 'Well,' he replied, 'it's a good idee'—he always pronounces the word 'idea' this way—'to have a sceptic in charge.'

'But why did you get involved in the programme if you don't expect it to find anything?' I asked.

I shall never forget his answer. It was a perfect example of being open to the world. Frank said, very simply but with obvious conviction: 'Because it's good science.'

It is strange—and I wouldn't necessarily have foreseen it—but a growing confidence in the reliability of the Christian story can actually awaken a person to the world outside the confines of their own head. They do not remain interested only in religion. Many people believe that Christianity stifles creative thought and makes people narrow-minded and afraid of new knowledge, but this is certainly not my observation. It can be true, but I have seen otherwise. The message of the Bible begins to convince people that they have value and meaning and that there is a living and personal God, and this allows them to explore and discover as well as to create. People don't flourish when they can't justify their actions with reasons that give them an ultimate purpose. This is very much the case with both discovery and creativity: we need a justification for both that is satisfying. Christianity, unlike so much of the competition in the marketplace of ideas, gives reason both to discover and to create. Both are necessary for human beings to flourish. We are not at the centre of the world: there is a reality outside ourselves as subjects. We don't make our own world alone, as individuals or as a culture. So, there is reason to discover. But it's also true that we are valuable and the image of God rests upon us, marred but ever present. We can affect the world around us and we have reason to do so. We have an internal world of desire that can be expressed. So, there is reason to create.

After several weeks of studying, on a different afternoon but in the same kitchen, the primary school teacher spoke to me with a slight, knowing smile. He admitted that he'd changed his mind. He now thought that an American who could find their country on an unmarked globe was a wealthier person for that knowledge. Though they might never have to find it in order to land the space shuttle, it was good and important for a person to know their relationship to the world.

This dynamic of learning and change flows many ways. A person may arrive wanting to tackle something theoretical and abstract but soon find themselves having to face instead something very personal, intimate and relational. Perhaps they find they can satisfy their gnawing intellectual doubt only by reconciling themselves to their past or to their family. However, it is also true that sometimes a person comes to L'Abri wanting to sort through an emotional problem, to receive something much more akin to counselling, and they are surprised to find that it's only by encountering reliable doctrine that they are able to escape from the pull of their deep emotional habits. In either case, it's a matter of having to face the world more honestly. Some people withdraw from reality into a safe academic thought-world and refuse to face their emotional life. But the retreat from the external world into the world of feelings can be just as real a withdrawal. This second kind of retreat is likewise a search for safety, as people refuse to encounter ideas that they can't control in the way they can their emotions.

It's very dangerous not to follow a curriculum but instead to try and go wherever a person needs to go. This is why prayer must be at the centre of what we are doing here rather than merely study. Our work requires the power of God at work in minds and hearts and circumstances.

I walked into the library on a cold, dark afternoon. I was meeting a new student from New Zealand for our first tutorial. She was already sitting on a couch with her feet curled up under her. Before I could introduce myself or say anything, she began: 'I've come here to have my nervous breakdown.' I shall never forget those words. They were said in a strong, clear voice, and I believed them. Her story was complicated, but she had previously undergone counselling at her church in which she was told she had suffered satanic ritual abuse as a child that she didn't remember. This is a fearsome diagnosis to make. I had no experience of it. She came from a background that overemphasized the activity of the demonic. Her church saw almost everything in terms of supernatural intervention, either by God or by demons. Human psychology and action were only the outworkings of this cosmic struggle. There was very little room to be human.

As I listened carefully to her, I realized that things didn't add up. I saw no evidence of ritual abuse in her life, and I slowly came to a different, no less fearsome, diagnosis that I very hesitantly term 'church abuse'. A theology that meant well had forced her to fit into its pattern. She was having a breakdown because she was trying to live with a false idea her church had given her, that people she loved had ritually abused her for occult purposes. She couldn't remember this happening, but she was told it was nevertheless true. As she tried to believe what her church taught her, she was forced into a very dark emotional place.

I was startled by how quickly her need for a nervous breakdown receded when we studied more carefully and with greater balance the unseen world as presented in the Bible. She was a real actor in her own life, not merely a stage on which God and Satan did battle. Sound theology helped to end her inner turmoil. I think we could have spent weeks talking about her emotional needs without seeing the freedom that a truer account of biblical teaching brought her.

However, because people are as complex as an image of God must be, the flow can also go in the opposite direction. A woman came to L'Abri very vocal in her distrust of the God of the Bible. In fact, she was unable to read the Bible, though her parents were missionaries in Brazil. It made her feel ill. On her very first night at the Manor it had been my turn to lecture. I explained how we approach the Bible in different ways and can come to it with very different expectations, very different 'pre-readings'. It isn't the world's most brilliant lecture, but I often give it near the beginning of a term because people seem to benefit from it. It accounts for a lot of misunderstandings we experience with one another in the church. On this night, however, when I finished, Claudia asked the first question. She used some expletives I'll omit, but her question was clear: 'What are you talking about for so long, and what difference does it make?'

Thankfully, I responded well to the challenge. The next morning at breakfast, rather than being the same angry, aggressive person she had been the night before, Claudia seemed embarrassed and ashamed of her behaviour. I assured her that she'd asked a perfectly acceptable question. She and I began to respect each other. We grew to know each other. Later that week, we sat under some apple trees in my garden that had been planted 15 years ago by another family. She was full of doctrinal questions and it was critical to get them answered right away. During the conversation I asked her several questions—and not least, 'Claudia, why are you asking these questions now?'

After she'd been with us for a term, she returned for another three months of study. She came to her second tutorial with six sheets of paper. We sat in the sunlight against a wall in the Sunken Garden. Each sheet was covered with scribbled questions that she wanted answered. They were, she told me, in no particular order. She also said that once she'd read them all to me the tutorial would be over. She didn't want to hear anything from me that day. As she read, I realized that they were theological questions but that the theme underlying them all seemed to be a profound distrust in God's care for her and his ability to protect her. When she came to her very last scribble, it wasn't actually a question, but it was something I had begun to suspect. During the previous summer holidays she had remembered that when she was a child her father had asked her to do inappropriate things to him. This was why she was asking all these questions now. Her theological enquiries and her distrust of God were real, but they were motivated by something more emotional than the questions at first suggested. The way forward for Claudia was to learn how to live with the awful reality of what had happened to her. She was tormented by shame.

At L'Abri we work half the day and study half the day. We don't just study, and we are not very good judges of when we are learning.

Each branch of L'Abri has a wonderful setting. Although we are not wealthy in terms of cash flow, you wouldn't know this to look at the places we inhabit. In Switzerland, the chalets are set on a steep hillside and look across the valley to a stunning chain of mountains that are forever changing colour. The Dutch branch is in an ancient farmhouse among apple orchards. They also have a big house on a canal next to the University of Utrecht. The Swedish L'Abri is on the green coast where the North Sea becomes the Baltic. On the Korean peninsula, the sun first rises on the mountains of the south near a resort, and this is where L'Abri is found in a large, wooden hotel. In America, the L'Abri houses in Rochester, Minnesota are perched on the summit of a hill with a vista of the city and its river below, and in Southborough, Massachusetts there is an old mansion set in woods. Finally, the most recent branch, in Canada, occupies a beautiful home among the trees and ponds of Bowen Island across from Vancouver. All the residential houses enjoy fantastic settings on very expensive real estate, and they all take a great deal of maintenance.

However, very few of us who live and work at L'Abri are good at maintenance, and those who are don't have enough time to do all the work required to keep (for example) an 18th-century manor house from crumbling slowly into the soil of Hampshire. Each branch, therefore, is a difficult place to live for those who love order and efficiency. We pray for people with special skills to come when we have a special need: roofers and plumbers and carpenters and computer programmers. If this sounds presumptuous or irresponsible, it isn't meant to be. These prayers have often been answered in a remarkable fashion—and what I appreciate most is that the usual answer comes in the form of a person who wants to lend us their skills rather than give us their money. Ken and Sally Phoenix, for example, after their retirement from teaching music in France and Germany began volunteering for whole terms at various branches. Ken can seemingly fix anything that is capable of breaking, and Sally brings a continental flair to our cuisine. They have been coming by for years to help us.

But everyone who comes to study, whether they think they are talented or not, needs to participate if the daily life of the community is to continue. There is, of course, all the cooking to be done, but the house is set in grounds that need mowing, while bathrooms need cleaning, gardens need sowing and weeding and harvesting and door frames need painting. Books must be reshelved if they are ever going to be found again, and someone has to chop wood if we want a cosy evening round the fire. Things do not happen automatically in a world in bondage to decay. It's an important lesson to learn about life in the universe.

Mistakes occur with so much amateur work going on: cakes fall instead of rise, rose bushes are pulled up instead of the weeds around them. There are lessons to be learned here as well. In fact, there is another dynamic we can observe. I remember that when I was studying science at university most of my classes had one section in the lecture hall and another in the laboratory. Because we were acquiring the skills and habits of science, we had to experience and establish in the laboratory the mysteries we were told about in the lectures. We were not merely to accept these things. We didn't consider that we knew something unless we understood it and could demonstrate it ourselves. Life is not so different: it isn't enough to excel only in the theory. And I continue to marvel at how often a student uses their study time to think about an issue and then has an opportunity to practise what they have learned. They listen to lectures or read books on a subject, and perhaps they begin to think they understand the idea; but then in the community, or during their work time, they are faced with a practical challenge to live it out. How many times have I seen someone study what the Bible says about forgiveness and then have to either forgive or be forgiven? It's much harder to hide in laboratory time.

Quite frequently, students are faced with their worst nightmare—the demand of laboratory time—in the form of another student living with us. In the early 1990s Eastern Europe was undergoing great changes as communist rule came to an end, and students from these countries were just beginning to come to study with us. The first Hungarian I ever met was a talented artist, very vivacious, and she lived up to my romantic notions of Bohemia. Dora told me that before coming to visit us in England she had actually prayed that she would have the chance to meet a Russian Christian. She wanted to talk through what had happened to her country with another believer.

However, English L'Abri had not had a Russian student in 20 years, not one, and I wasn't hopeful that her prayer would be answered. Dora slept in a top bunk and, a few weeks later, beneath her slept Natasha, our first Russian student. They had a lot to talk about, and it wasn't easy for either of them. It wasn't until Natasha met Dora that she learned the truth that Russian tanks didn't come to liberate Hungary in 1956 but to perpetuate its repression. Natasha's world tilted, and Dora found herself helping the Russian to grieve rather than venting her own anger as she had expected. This could not have been accomplished merely by reading tales of reconciliation.

This is one of the major reasons that we do L'Abri while living together. We are committed to the importance of ideas, but we don't think that disembodied knowledge is the goal.

Work is important. We don't do the least amount of work we can to win the weekend's leisure. Very few people have the ability to study all day, and even if they can it is of very doubtful profit. It is far better to learn a lesson well and then live out that lesson than it is to conquer material partially and move on to the next tape or lecture. That, in fact, is closer to the definition of vanity than to learning. We work together and can discuss what we are thinking. We work alone and can reflect on our studies.

Actually, we are very poor judges of when we are learning. This is partly because we prejudge certain forms of behaviour as 'learning'. If we sit quietly underlining words on a page or taking notes while we listen to someone else speak, we are likely to say we are studying. We may say we learned from that study if we can repeat some of the words back on request.

Dick Keyes, a colleague in L'Abri working in Massachusetts, has observed how often Jesus asked questions of people as he travelled. And apparently one of the most frequent questions he asked was 'Haven't you read the scriptures?' He asked this of people who had spent their lives poring over the writings of the prophets. Of course they had read the scriptures! What he meant was, 'You think you have read the scriptures. Can you see that this situation reveals that you haven't learned?' The scholars and experts in the law were irritated by the question. A wise person recognizes such an irritation as an opportunity to learn.

Sometimes we can't grasp an idea until we have seen it expressed in some concrete way. And, even more frequently today, we can't even acknowledge that we believe in an idea until we ourselves have made it tangible somehow.

In lieu of a real maintenance person, Andrew does the best he can overseeing things around the Manor. It's surprising how often he gives just the right job to just the right person—for that person's sake as well as the job's. Matthew was a jazz guitarist from a band in Seattle who came to study with us after he tired of life on the road. Some of the old walls around the property were on the brink of falling down and so Andrew assigned Matthew the task of repointing them—that is, removing the ivy and replacing the worn mortar between the stones. Matthew had never done a task like this, but he threw himself into it and was making real headway. But then someone from our local parish council stopped by to complain about the repairs. The colour of the new mortar didn't match the old, and the villagers who had to look at it every day didn't appreciate the quality of the work. No account was taken of how much Matthew had learned, how hard he was trying or how little money we had (which ruled out paying for professional help).

However, an expert from the council did come round to give us some materials and some helpful advice. And, though Matthew had to undo most of the work he had already completed, he managed to maintain a good attitude. Better than that, he actually saw positive value in the experience. Andrew was his tutor and they had been talking about the walls Matthew had constructed in his life. It may sound trite, but the metaphor was powerful and kept recurring in their conversations together. The old walls, constructed for self-protection and without dependence on God, were still standing, but they obviously had no real strength. Matthew's task was not merely to repair these old structures but to make a proper job of them, using the correct materials and being patient until he got them right. The rough walls of the Manor are things he can run his hands over and he has said that they've helped him to understand the ones he created himself but couldn't see.

Each term we try to have one or two workdays, when we break our ordinary schedules and all work together on a larger project that has been neglected because it isn't urgently required for daily life. Sometimes a wit will remark that we have quite a racket going for us at the Manor, getting people to pay to stay with us and then getting them to work for our benefit. This is how Andrew managed to recover the Sunken Garden.

There was a small field beneath the Manor's southern windows where we hung our washing lines. It was an ugly spot for which we showed little care, but we did keep noticing bricks and pavements and patterns in the grass. We decided to investigate this, and it was not unlike doing archaeology. We kept finding new surprises: there were cobblestones and millstones, and some of the bricks outlined what had been a long pool running the length of it. Andrew decided to reclaim the area and return it to being a formal English garden. It was the toil of every workday for a couple of years. There were tree stumps to pull out of the ground, prising their tenacious fingers out of the soil—never a pleasant task. And there were tons of rubble to remove, which had to be sorted by hand into the ironstone, which we could sell to builders, and the old, broken bricks we needed to use as filler elsewhere on the property or had to haul away to the dump. Sometimes the students would complain—though rarely seriously—that they were working to create something beautiful for future generations of L'Abri students but that they themselves were never going to get to appreciate it.

If they didn't enjoy this time together reclaiming something lost or doing the groundwork to make something for the future, I suppose they were technically correct. However, I find that this is so often the way with even very valuable labour. In John 4, Jesus tells his disciples that the fields they reap in (so ripe for harvest!) were worked long and hard by other people before them, people who were faithful to the task though they had little hope of seeing any reward in their day.

The Sunken Garden is now a lovely, quiet spot in the grounds haunted by people who need a little respite from the constant conversation around the house. It is also used by the children for paper-boat races. A visitor from the University of California at Davis one summer made a fascinating zoo for us from the various creatures that had made their home in the pond. And every once in a while a student who is a veteran from those thankless workdays, when it was more like slaving for the Pharaoh than having fun, drops by for a visit. They usually go out to the garden, and their sense of satisfaction at a change for the better in the world, a change in which they played a part, even a small part, is very encouraging.

# Equally Yoked

*"People are looking at us to see if when we say we have truth, it is then possible for this truth not only to take men's souls to Heaven, but to give all of life meaning in the present time, moment by moment."*

Francis Schaeffer

Is L'Abri after all a community?

Our vocation is not primarily to create a community together. We view our task as serving the people sent to us by God—as I have said previously, 'to show forth by demonstration in our lives and work the existence of God'. This vague but demanding brief can be carried out in many ways. Lunchtime discussions and lectures for students living with us are what we do, but the demonstration can go down other avenues. God could lead us in other directions. Our purpose is not to live together for its own sake, or for our own support or comfort. Rather, we share a common task—and this task is done best if we live life together. God is often best seen by the fruit of his Spirit growing in his people. Our community is a means and not an end; but this doesn't diminish the importance of our fellowship together, because means do matter. In fact, if I was allowed to nominate one sermon that all the clergy of every church and denomination, in every culture and context, had to read, I would require them all to read one by Schaeffer entitled 'The Lord's work in the Lord's way'. It pays a great deal of attention to the means we use to achieve a goal.

When we contemplate living and working with other
believers, we must be honest and not romantic. We shouldn't
be either cynical or utopian. There are blessings and there are
difficulties. At English L'Abri, the workers gather together for
a meeting every Tuesday during term-time. This lasts most of
the morning, and it is here that we discuss everyone's concerns.
Some may be very important and others may be less weighty.
The first difficulty we face, of course, is that we don't always
agree on which category an issue falls into. When the Curry
family's bitch comes into heat, the Fellow family's male dog takes
to sleeping across the threshold of the Currys' house. Does this
sound a trivial matter? Do you think this can't cause real friction
within a group of Christians working together? If you think it is
unimportant, you're being naive and otherworldly.

We don't raise each other's children. Each family is like a
separate nation with its own legal code. Nevertheless, we are
hugely involved with each other and we influence one another.
Fiona Bradshaw is very aware if another family allows their
seven-year-old to watch *The Lord of the Rings* before she is
allowed to. It seems an injustice to her. And when our children
argue with each other, as they do, the other families view this
from different perspectives.

Not everyone at the Manor has a pet or children or is
married. A single worker goes to their flat in the evening as
tired as a married worker. The single sister knows, but can't fully
understand, that the married brother goes home to children
grumpy from the day's disappointments. The married worker
knows, but doesn't fully understand, how hard it is to be single
and to have no one on the pillow next to you to talk to about
the day's disappointments. All of us naturally think that our
situation is misunderstood and the harder to bear.

We don't have to be each other's best friend to live and work
together. This may come as a surprise. Friendship is what many
people expect when they begin a community together. They love
each other as friends and they want this relationship to become

ever deeper and more intimate. Yet that expectation can actually be the beginning of the death of a community of Christians working together. It isn't natural affinities that bind us to one another. Such natural friendships are a thing of great beauty; but of course they really do nothing special to demonstrate God's existence and his activity to change lives. Some of us have a natural liking for others in the branch, or just as often we feel naturally irritated by other colleagues; but we are bound together in our common service to Jesus Christ and we have decided to serve him in a particular way. God's existence is demonstrated best when we love each other and serve each other in spite of our natural reactions. Our world does need to see the marvel of friendship modelled before its eyes—especially non-sexual friendships—but it also must see that we can rise above our natural inclinations. Jesus encouraged us to invite to dinner those who couldn't return the invitation.

We don't have to be best friends. We do have to trust and respect one another. We have to be able to be honest, both in affirming and in confronting each other. Both are necessary, but there is nothing more difficult. We must wish each other well and not be jealous if the students seem to appreciate another colleague more than us. We must not secretly enjoy the failure of another brother or sister because this makes us look better than them. Everyone knows that the vast majority of missionaries who abandon their work do so because of what we call 'personality conflicts'.

Some of us travel and speak in exotic places and prestigious circumstances. These individuals become in demand: people clamour for them. When someone calls the Manor, you can tell they don't want to speak to you, they want to talk to your better-known colleague. We have to recognize that we have different gifts and opportunities. Relative fame is not always fair or deserved. And yet we are actually equal in value, though all external indicators say otherwise. Nothing is more difficult than living in the reality of this and refusing the temptation to undervalue ourselves or to despise the public success of a fellow worker. These same temptations of course plague any local church, but they are intensified by our life together in L'Abri.

We pray for God's guidance. We 'tarry for one another' in decision-making. It is not a way of doing things designed for immediate efficiency. Some of us, of course, value achievements more highly than others. Some of us value warm personal relationships more than activity and attaining goals. A few of us like meetings; a few of us see meetings as a barely necessary evil. We don't always agree on what the wise way ahead is in a particular situation. When are a minority and its concerns or anxieties allowed to frustrate the will of the majority? There isn't a rule for this, a system designed to make things easier. Instead there is wisdom and discernment.

It is a sad reality that I observe frequently that it's the people who know us best who don't allow us to change. This may be in part because at first taking a new direction is like learning a new role in a play, trying to imagine ourselves differently. We may be very serious about it, but to begin with it always looks like a kind of game. The new costume doesn't seem to fit us as well as our old clothes. We're trying to assume a new characteristic, and so at the very outset it isn't really true. It can be criticized. We can be criticized. The reason for this criticism may not be that the change is a bad thing. Those who know us may have been telling us for a long time that they wish we would change in this very way. They may have been praying for this change to occur. But when we embark on it, when we begin to see that the change is possible and we start living in the new way, those who know us are right to say, 'Who are you trying to fool? You aren't that way. You're pretending. Stop pretending and *really* change!'

They are right to say this in that the new us isn't actually us yet. The criticism is accurate. But they are wrong to say it in that they are crushing the early beginnings of what would develop into a real change in our character. The first steps in being newly obedient to God or newly trusting him will look uncoordinated, just as a person looks when after months of physical therapy they finally struggle out of their wheelchair. This is true even of works that God's Spirit is accomplishing. People who know us—even people who claim to wish us well—can inhibit us from actually changing. Think how the villagers who had known Jesus as a child attempted with this knowledge to prevent him from being a rabbi, a prophet, the Messiah. And yet they would have claimed to love rabbis and prophets and to be eagerly awaiting the Messiah.

This inhibition of growth happens in families. It can also happen between Christians living and working together. It can happen at church. This is in spite of the fact that both families and Christian communities are meant to be places that prompt and support change and foster maturity. When it acts in this way, a community is its own enemy and the enemy of its members.

Not only can we frustrate real change, we can also cut unspoken deals with each other. Over time we get to know each other well. We see each other's weaknesses, we see where there needs to be growth. But change and growth—becoming conformed to the image of Christ[7]—are not a pleasant process. I see where you must grow. You see where I must grow. We both realize that this entails inconvenience and pain. And so we cut an unspoken deal: 'I won't expect you to change if you won't expect me to.' At this point, we have stopped loving one another and wishing the best for each other. This must be a form of grieving the Holy Spirit.

The blessing of living and working together is that it doesn't have to be this way. We must not be idealists. Our dreams of perfect fellowship can be the enemy of the real thing. We can't expect our fellowship to escape the temptations to envy, to inhibit change, to cut unspoken deals. We shall fail at times—but when we realize that we have made such an unloving contract we can break it, or, better still, invite the other person to break

[7] Romans 8:29

it with us. When we see that we have stopped hoping for real change in a brother or sister, even though we talk about it all the time, we can start imagining with them the first stages of the change. When we are tempted we don't have to sin, even if we have sinned in the past.

We try to live this way at L'Abri. We invite people to live with us, and they watch us. So, of course, we fall into the trap of doing it *because* people are watching, rather than letting people observe what we are doing for God's pleasure. If I play Frisbee on a chilly evening out behind the Manor with my daughters, I know that the students who are eating in the dining room can see us on the lawn. It's very important for them to see a father play with his children, and we make a very picturesque scene. So, I'm tempted to be self-aware and play with my children primarily because the students are watching. There's no way around this temptation, and yet I ought to play Frisbee in spite of it. I should do it even if no one but God is watching.

When my wife and I came to England in the hope of working with L'Abri, I had three questions I asked many people. The first was: 'Isn't this a kind of ministry that has had its day? Shouldn't L'Abri have died with Schaeffer?' And sometimes visitors do come and criticize us. Usually there is some reference to ageing hippies living on a commune. The answer I got to my question, however, was that living together to study and pray and proclaim the message of the Bible is a 'method' more needed now than even back in the 1960s and '70s. Society has only continued to decay. Technology allows people to be in contact with one another every hour of every day, but they feel as alienated and alone as ever. Culture has, for the most part, grown only more distant from the will of the Creator. There are today more and more communities beginning as study centres that are not associated with L'Abri, and this is encouraging. We have always told people not to try and start a L'Abri but to take whatever they have benefited from in their experience with us and translate it into their own environment. L'Abri has never been ambitious for growth *per se*.

Today, most of the young adults who come and live with us are dissatisfied by their experience of church, and this disaffection is alarming in its depth and its breadth. It's alarming to us at L'Abri because we are an organization that loves the Church and sees the local congregation of the universal Body of Christ as the place where God is best honoured and the usual locus of his work in human lives. This dissatisfaction is understandable and some of its causes are just. The local congregation can lack reality. Its words can far outstrip its behaviour. Evangelical churches in particular, in their commitment to preaching the unchanging gospel, can sometimes give the impression that our tastes and our interests should be similarly ancient and changeless. Inadvertently we communicate an innate conservatism rather than the revolution of God's kingdom.

As with prayer, people are experimenting today in how to 'do church', looking for creative ways to make the congregation fit into our culture and its pace and patterns. We want it to feel real to us and to be attractive to our neighbours. The Sunday morning routine we grew up with can seem like something from the 19th century. Not all, but many people who come to L'Abri find us a much more satisfying experience than their church. In comparison, we get to know one another here quickly because we live with each other. We see each other in different situations and not just at a worship service. We have the opportunity to work together, and we spend hours in conversation on all sorts of topics. We rely on God together in prayer, and the institution seems so fragile that we can't assume that it would survive if the Living God were to cease to exist. By contrast, the church looks set to roll on whether or not God is involved and we make the mistake of thinking that its momentum can be explained in terms of sociology and psychology alone.

Many kinds of people come to L'Abri. There is a diversity of accent and hairstyle. It makes for a wonderful heterogeneity, which often makes people's home churches look dull and beige. And there are non-Christians present, though they are rarely in the majority, and they're allowed to rattle the cage and disagree. These things lead our students to think that their churches need to be more like L'Abri.

English L'Abri has started three local churches during its three decades, and all three continue to this day. We do have people visit and insist that we are actually a church ourselves. We deny this, however. The Reformers had various definitions of the church, but usually they revolved around the three 'signs' of the preaching of the word of God, the celebration of the sacraments and the biblical discipline of the believers. L'Abri is a servant of the church. All our workers are to be part of and submitted to a Bible-teaching congregation.

I used to think that L'Abri existed only because local churches didn't do all that they ought to and that if the church was healthy there would be no need for L'Abri. My opinions have altered on this. Sometimes it takes a little distance for us to see things in perspective. When we travel and live among strangers we may find it helps us in our quest for answers and changes. There are some questions that are very hard to ask among people who know you and who you have to get on with.

One of the major teachings of Schaeffer was that in the gospel of Jesus and the power of God's Spirit there is the possibility for 'supernaturally restored relationships'. This means that people can change, that they are allowed to change, and that painful broken relationships that are hopeless in the view of psychology can recover. This is one of the most difficult things to experience, because we have a part to play in the restoration even though it is supernatural. We have to trust God enough to stop living by the methods we have practised all our lives. I have seen this happen many times. No relationships are ever perfect, but they can be substantially restored. And they can be seen to be restored. These are real-world, observable changes, not something that takes place only in an invisible realm.

We can experience this substantial healing of our broken relationships with one another because we ourselves have been healed and forgiven and reconciled to the Living God. This relationship with God can't be seen, though it has a myriad of manifestations—among which is the restoration of our human relationships. It is no use protesting that we love the unseen God when we don't love the brothers or sisters who we see around us.[8] If the power of the gospel cannot be seen to restore human relationships, why should we expect people to believe us when we insist that it restores a very broken relationship with God?

We teach this, and it is a source of pain to me. I'm aware of how often I am living in continuing violation of this claim. It's easy to speak passionately about these things while actually living with broken relationships with our family and our colleagues. I refuse to trust God and I embrace my habits of selfishness instead. I think these will protect me from disappointment. They can wear a thousand different faces. I find myself very subtly discouraging a colleague from growing and changing because this would challenge me and reveal my own darkness. I harbour suspicion and anger. I pretend to agree with people when I don't for the sake of a false peace rather than fighting for a real one. Uncharitable thoughts plague me. This is the hardest part of living together.

But we have one another for a reason. We may need help and arbitration. Being reconciled with one another, forgiving one another, wishing the best for one another—these things are not glamorous or romantic. But they demonstrate that Jesus Christ reconciles people to God and to one another.

[8] See 1 John 3.

# When Art Is Not a Luxury

*"If it is true that philosophy, the first step in the line of despair, touched only a few people, art, the second step, influenced very many more."*
Francis Schaeffer

The two friends were unlikely companions in many ways because they were so different, but they understood that in a friend one isn't looking for one's self. On an afternoon midway through September, they were walking through the Blackmoor orchards talking of this and that.

Whump!

'What was that?' the first man asked, turning round, seeking the source of the noise.

'Just an apple falling,' said the second, not bothering to turn.

The first man went back and bent over the apple. 'That's strange,' he remarked.

His friend paused. 'No, it's not.' His voice gave a hint of irritation. 'They all do that.'

'Yes,' the first man said slowly. He squatted and picked up the apple with care. 'But why do they do that?' He stood and looked up at the branch from which it must have dropped.

The apple had a leaf still attached to its stem. The afternoon light came through the branches, dappling everything. As the first man looked up, he held the apple and its leaf in his hand and they glowed in the orange light. The second man walked back to where his friend stood, but he didn't look up. He stared at the apple. 'Would you look at that!' he said, a new tone in his voice.

'What?' asked the first distractedly.

'This apple. Look at this apple!' replied the second.

'Yes, they all look that way,' said the first, not seeming to notice that his friend had taken the apple from his hand.

The second man held it up and turned it around, never taking his eyes from it. 'No, they don't,' he said. 'None of them look like this one.' His voice grew in confidence. 'No apple that has ever existed before has looked like this particular one.'

A couple of years ago at Dutch L'Abri, an artist who was studying there led the students in a workshop. They divided into pairs. Each person had a sheet of paper before them and a pen. The exercise they were given to do was to look at their partner and draw their face without once either glancing down at their paper or lifting their pen from it. Of course, people protested at first. It sounded threatening. It gave them every opportunity to fail. They weren't proper artists. They gave lots of excuses, but then everyone tried the experiment. It is very intimate to gaze at someone's face with the intention of really seeing it: to follow the curve of their nostrils, the asymmetry of their lips. Rob Ludwick, who works at Dutch L'Abri, told me it was even uncomfortably intimate to do this exercise with Christa, his wife.

If the drawers had looked at their paper, they would have drawn what they expected a face to look like. They would have paid less attention to the unique face sitting across from them. When they had finished, none of their drawings resembled their models. They looked more like something Picasso might have done. Things were not in proportion, the eyes might smear onto the same side of the face, the forehead didn't go with the chin. But on a closer and slower inspection the likenesses began to emerge. The different features did coalesce into a familiar face. You might even say that something more real of each face had been caught than if the drawers had drawn more conventionally.

It's an experiment you might try. They do it once a term now at Dutch L'Abri.

Art has always been part of the heritage of L'Abri, and there are probably two reasons for this. First, as Schaeffer tried to understand his day and tried to proclaim the message of the Bible to the people of that day, he found that the arts were a rich source of understanding of what people were thinking in the society he lived in. He found that you could see their ideas, and the results of their ideas, in what they produced. Philosophies and worldviews do not remain mere abstractions: they become novels and films, paintings and pieces of music, performances and installations. Ideas are manifested in behaviour and law. By paying serious attention to art, Schaeffer showed his respect for what the people around him were saying in the confusion and pain of the 20th century.

I was in art school during the 1970s. I had never heard of Schaeffer. My church had never addressed an issue through the medium of art and had never addressed the issues that faced us in our art. I knew that something was wrong. There was friction between my Christian intuitions and the things my teachers were saying. It was like one of those noises you hear while driving your car. The squeak is quiet at first, but it's no good just ignoring it. The sound grows more insistent. Where is it coming from? What on earth is causing it? You don't know what it is, but you're sure it's not meant to be there.

But I had no help in finding the source of this friction, and in the end I dropped out of my studies. If I had encountered Christians who understood the language of art and the tensions of the day, I might have been able to remain in art school. Perhaps that would have been a good thing, perhaps not. But my religious background had done nothing to make me a productive, creative member of society. For the most part, it had been interested solely in making sure that I obtained forgiveness

for my sins—and refrained from the more blatant iniquities of
my generation. It also taught that I should be responsible and do
my duty. These are not small things, of course—in fact, they are
vital. But they're not the whole of the reality that Christ is Lord
over. I saw culture primarily in terms of ethics: it could be right
or wrong, moral or immoral, it could degenerate or improve.
That is an opinion I still hold, though it's very unpopular and
offensive now in an age that generally regards culture as the
thing that determines ethics and invents right and wrong. I think
we can still ask ethical questions of culture. Nonetheless, it's not
enough to judge a culture by its moral goodness. A culture ought
also to cause human beings to flourish, to be creative, to begin
showing the glory that is part of being in God's image, to begin
showing the glory that is going to be revealed finally and wholly
in the Kingdom of God. We are not only going to be good in
Heaven; we are going to be interesting.

This is the second reason for the interest in art. People
are communicating today, and I should stop and listen. But I
am also a person of my day, I have a voice and I, too, want to
communicate. I want to speak to others, and the words of a
sermon are not the only way to speak. I want to worship God,
and the words of a hymn are not the only way to worship. I want
to express my own interaction with the world. I wish to groan
a faithful groan at the decay around me in a world cursed and
frustrated.[9] I want to sing in joy at the evidence of glory I can
already see around me and in me.[10]

Art is not a luxury, though much of the ludicrously expensive
art of the institutions and the high-art industry may be. 'Art
needs no justification' is the way Hans Rookmaaker put it, and
this is one of those sayings we have come to repeat over and over
again at L'Abri. By this he didn't mean that art is autonomous, or
'art for art's sake'. He meant that engaging in the arts as a creator
or an enjoyer is a good human activity. Further 'justifying

[9] Romans 8:20–23
[10] Psalm 72:19

reasons' are unnecessary. Being a Christian doesn't mean having
to switch off one's intellect; nor does it mean having to switch off
one's imagination. After all, hope—one of the identifiers of those
who follow Jesus—is largely a matter of being able to imagine
that good is going to destroy evil, that all that is mortal will be
swallowed up by life.[11] We do not see this: we hope for it, we
eagerly await it, we imagine it. It's only right that we should help
other people to grow imaginative.

The evangelical church has come a long way since I was in art
school. Christian organizations today have people dedicated to
ministering to arts students so that they can resolve the tensions
I faced. There are mentoring groups for practising artists who
are Christians, somewhere they can gather and critique each
other's work and encourage each other amidst the harsh realities
of making a career. Some Christian journals have regular
contributors considering the world of contemporary art. There
are churches in east London and elsewhere that have a particular
vision to reach out to the arts community locally. Christian
colleges in America offer drama programmes that their Puritan
forebears would have regarded with deep suspicion. And it
isn't all just Christians working for and with other Christians. I
know of people who are very anxious not to be coddled in a safe
environment but instead want their art to be an invitation to the
whole of society to engage in discourse. There is good reason to
feel that progress has been made. Certainly many artists today
are interested in considering 'spiritual' issues—though even
they may sometimes be prejudiced against a Christian voice.
Things have improved, but many perennial questions still plague
Christian as creators or enjoyers of art.

We must be careful here. We can cause unnecessary
problems. Much of the fine arts in their fascination with
concepts has reached a dead end. This is not a Christian
judgement, it is a judgement the art world itself has made. This
was admitted in the notes written by the curator of the 2003

[11] 2 Corinthians 5:4

Biennale (the largest art show in Europe, which takes place in Venice).

> Art survives as its caricature. Its charm actually lies in its irrelevance. Everything concerning it is a justification of its gratuitousness. Its arbitrary values confirm the fact that they are vacuous. Art is a circensian mode of expression. Many people believe that professionalism demonstrated in the making of an artwork can justify its uselessness. Artists knowingly accept the responsibility of producing the buffoonery people find amusing. Rather than being embarrassed each finds the way to think he or she is the best. Artists never manage to relate to the world, but only to their own presumption. Their merit consists in sad acceptance of the rules governing consideration of their ability.
>
> You can buy yourself a catalogue and watch it age on the shelf along with what you believed. We are all intent upon our wondrous biennalious labours, but the true subject of an artwork is its obsolescence. Every generation is derided by the next. Art is not about human expressive capacity but its conditioning; because art is a way to capitalize wealth. It is presumed to be exceptional, helping people to resign themselves to the dullness of normality. Luck be with you, viewer.

Art can be at a dead end when it becomes only criticism and cannot point to a way out. There is a place for artists to tweak the nose of society, to wave a red flag in the face of accepted conventions if these are destructive, to remind us to look at things we'd prefer not to see. But a criticism that never stops criticizing to move on to say something positive is like an after-dinner speaker who clears his throat—and then carries on clearing his throat, with nothing further to say. It's wise to clear your throat before speaking, but the audience is right to expect something more. Christian artists can fall into this same trap (and so can Christian theologians). They can be so sensitive to the criticism that Christians refuse to face the horrors of existence that they begin to suspect that hope is a cop-out, that only cynicism is honest.

We had a group of student film-makers down for a weekend at the Manor. They were each earnestly committed to their work 'being about reality'; but when they were asked what they meant by this, it became clear that they meant they wanted to show the shocking, painful aspects of reality. They were shocked themselves when over the weekend we accused them of unreality, but their work was partial. For example, it didn't acknowledge that a Hindu mother in a drought-stricken village breast-feeding her infant even at the cost of her own health was a story of beauty as well as horror. They refused to acknowledge the existence of beauty. Their view of reality was just as inadequate as that of those people who always insist on a happy ending.

This is very much the point of Robert Altman's film *The Player*. This is a movie about Hollywood and the making of movies. Two artists want to make a film without stars and without a happy ending. 'This is not an American film,' says one of the characters. The hero of their screenplay is a prosecuting attorney who falls in love with a woman who is due to die in the gas chamber after he has proved her guilt. He then labours to prove her innocence and when he succeeds he runs to the prison only to find that the execution has already been carried out. 'This is reality,' one of the artists declares as he finishes pitching the story to the studio executive played by Tim Robbins, who listens to 30,000 stories a year though only a dozen of them will ever be made into movies. The screenplay may sound like a tragedy but it functions in Altman's film as a piece of satire, making fun of artistic pretensions that insist that only in a relentless tale of crushing disappointment are we being honest about life. I won't give the ending away.

Art will not remain at a dead end, just as history didn't finish with the end of the Cold War. Human beings are incorrigibly creative. There will be further reactions. We must be very careful when we talk of a dead end, especially as Christians. Let me give you an example that puts me in a bad light. The Turner Prize is the award for British visual arts that receives the most media attention. Recently it has generally gone to an artist whose work as shown is controversial and perceived by most of those outside the arts community as strange or insulting. In 2001, Madonna came to present the prize to Martin Creed. The award is given for more than just one piece of work, but the piece by Creed on display was entitled *The Lights Going On and Off*. It was an empty gallery in which lights flashed on and off at five-second intervals. It was minimalistic; it was 'the postmodern gesture'.

I thought it was a sad dead-end and I predicted (albeit not very seriously) that there were only two years of Turner prizes left. In 2002 they would put a sack over your head and lead you through a gallery. At the other end they would take it off and you wouldn't know if the lights in the gallery had been on or off. And then 2003 would see the final prize. This year you would walk through an empty gallery in total darkness. There would be a handrail to hold on to, but this would be only for insurance purposes. Art would have reached its end.

So I spoke: criticizing, though from a position I meant to be sympathetic. However, we had an artist—an organist—come and study with us briefly, wanting to learn from us about art and the Christian faith and how the two related. We spoke of the Turner Prize. I thought I was being helpful. Instead, he taught me.

'No, you're missing the point,' he said, the words tumbling out under the pressure of frustration. 'I think Creed's work is beautiful.'

I was very surprised and asked him how it could be.

'To my generation, it's a gesture full of meaning,' he answered. 'We've forgotten that light and darkness are not the same thing. It would be a very powerful thing to stand in that empty gallery and suddenly realize that light and dark are different.'

Creed himself said of the piece in an interview: 'People can make of it what they like. I don't think it is for me to explain it.' Maybe he was making fun of his audience. He merely wired up a timer to the room's lights and left. He didn't even have to stay and flip the switch. People who assume that that is his attitude think he is making fun of them and are angry. But maybe he actually loves his audience and wishes them well. I can't really say.

The church and her progress in the arts may be a lot like me. Perhaps we have learned to feel love for those around us who are showing their frustration and sense of meaninglessness and their inability to imagine a good future. But this sympathy is not the end of the process: we have to do the hard work of listening with ears not our own. Rather than a dead end, as I suspected, perhaps for some Creed's work could be a beginning. Certainly in Genesis the distinction made between the light and the darkness was very much at the beginning of everything.

One of the chronic tensions still felt between Christian artists and their churches is over the need for a message in their work. Having learned that art can communicate powerfully, and having grown more confident that creativity is an aspect of being human that the Living God affirms, the church wants Christian artists to use their work to preach the gospel. Or else, since her own message is one of hope, she wants their work to give comfort and to be pretty and pleasing. These expectations seem reasonable and devout to the church, but to many who wish to create they seem constrictive. I think of the lyrics of a popular song by the band The 2nd Chapter of Acts, sung in the days when 'contemporary Christian music' was just beginning to burgeon: 'You ask me why I (only) sing about Jesus, and I answer because Jesus is my song.'

Following this logic, I have had artists tell me that they don't want to believe in Jesus because this would end their freedom and oblige them to follow a different path to the one their art was leading them on. I've also spoken with Christian artists who are afraid that their faith will turn their work into feeble propaganda. I give the same reply to Christians and non-Christians, and I think this is a good sign. It is true that belief in the God of the Bible will impose boundaries on one's art. There is no getting around this, and if total freedom is the absolute goal, the artist must realize that the Christian gospel is their adversary.

Most, however, do not realize where these boundaries lie. First, the artist must love their audience. That is a necessity, a hard boundary. Much art makes me feel that I'm hated by the artist. This love, however, has nothing to do with making only work that makes people feel warm and comfortable and safe. Think of the prophets and the apostles: it is a very loving thing at times to trouble and disturb your audience. There will be times to comfort the heartbroken and times to upset the complacent.

And an artist must be honest in their message. This is a second boundary: one mustn't lie. It was Henry James, I think, who said that the job of the novelist was to show the demons in his angels and the angels in his demons. This makes sense, of course: people are highly complicated. Every one has in them value and potential, every one has in them sin and the stupidity of evil. But this kind of complexity is very different from saying (for example) that rape is a beautiful thing. We can never say that rape is beautiful. This doesn't mean that we have to be predictable, or speak only in clichés, or always have to be frightfully clear and unambiguous. Robert Beningni's film *Life is Beautiful* was a controversial portrayal of the Holocaust through a game a father was playing with his little boy. I think it did a great job. It made me feel anew a horror that was only too familiar to me through so many images and stories. It made my wife cry more than the much more graphic account of Steven Spielberg's *Schindler's List*.

And an artist must be humble in their attitude. They may make a mirror for us to look into or they may make a window through which we can see out onto the world outside. They may be very intimate and revealing and autobiographical—this book itself comes very close to being self-referential—yet they must never insist on being at the centre of the universe. This is hardest perhaps for those who perform in various ways, because the audience wants to put them briefly at the centre of things. This is the third boundary the gospel imposes on the artist: focus on what you will, but remember that you are not in reality at the very centre.

These three principles—love of the audience, honesty and humility—does anyone seriously want to violate these? If so, then the gospel will inhibit your work. If not, however, you may be surprised at how free you are. And of course all three actually implode into love of self, love of neighbour and love of God—the summation of the Law, nothing more and nothing less.

However, it's not only loss of freedom that artists fear from Christianity: they also fear loss of power. Again, I hear this both from artists who believe in Jesus and from those who do not: 'If I allow this news of reconciliation with God to permeate my life, and I find myself hopeful, I shall lose the very thing that fuels my work.' This sounds strange in the ears of many, but please realize that this is important to artists. These people believe that only despair can make fine art. Looking back over history, they demand, which of the 'greats' was happy?

This is a very serious, indeed a catastrophic, mistake to make, and the church must recognize its allure for artists. However, I can say with the volume turned all the way up to 10 that hope is a better fuel than despair. Hope is an imagination of how the world can be and, if that hope is true, how the world will be. It is a foundation on which we can build, within the boundaries of love. It is a great perspective from which to be critical, for it is when we know that things can be better that we have a vantage-point from which to denounce the ugly. It allows us to build with more than criticism. We can stop clearing our throats and can go further. Parents, out of love, sometimes have to criticize their children; but it would be a poor parent who only criticized. That would become a boring and destructive sound in the ears of a child. A parent has hope for their child, and that is why they sometimes criticize.

I had a friend who was very gifted. He was creative in many areas we recognize as art. He began as a student at L'Abri, but my family came to love him and so later he would just flow in and out of our lives as he travelled. He was very unpredictable, because social conventions meant little to him; yet love meant a great deal to him and because of this he was easily misunderstood as immoral and irresponsible, whereas I consider him one of the most moral people I have met. It was he who first really argued with me that he had to retain his despair and depression because it was these that gave him his creative energy. I was still not clear about these things myself. I could tell that something was fundamentally wrong with his attitude, but I couldn't persuade him by showing him a better way. And this friend did commit suicide. The despair and depression, at first seen by him as a help of sorts, a precondition for creativity, overwhelmed him. He forgot that there was reason to hope, and so he put an end to all his earthly creativity. I knew that what we had spoken about was important, but I hadn't realized until then that it was a matter of life and death.

# Behind Your Sunglasses and Between Your Headphones

*"We are to put everything second so we can be alive to the voice of God and allow Him to speak to us and confront us."*

Francis Schaeffer

Each student is assigned a tutor for the time they are at L'Abri. This doesn't mean they can't speak with whoever they wish to, of course, but it does mean that everyone has someone in particular looking out for them. We have lunchtime conversations almost every day, and we have lectures at least three times a week, and these are public opportunities to consider current ideas. However, people also need private opportunities to speak about their thoughts. Some issues are just too sensitive to put on display among people you don't know and who don't know you. Eloquent extroverts should not receive all the attention at a Christian study centre. And because we don't have a curriculum that everyone goes through, each student needs to talk through what they are learning. They need a conversation that isn't blown off course by another, more powerful personality and their favourite topic, and they need a conversation that takes their own background seriously. There are no abstract questions because each question is asked by a particular human being.

This can seem to place an enormous and wholly unrealistic burden of expectation on the L'Abri workers. We are not truly intellectuals, and we cannot possibly engage expertly with every

issue the students may seek help with. We are not intellectuals—
and yet we do share a lively curiosity about the world and about
the cultures that people create and inhabit.

Dawn told me about a time when she felt her inadequacy.
She went into the office and looked at the list of students and
tutors. Andrew had placed next to her name a new arrival, a
woman down from a British university who was in the throes
of a PhD in one of the physical sciences. Dawn herself has not
completed a university degree, and she felt intimidated by the
assignment. A flood of worries overtook her. What does religion
have to say to science today? How was she to impress this
woman when she had no credentials? Dawn is very cunning in
some ways, and she told me that for their first conversation she
arranged with the visiting scientist to go for a walk down Church
Lane. This would look natural, but the thinking behind it was
that Dawn didn't want to be sitting across from the woman in an
armchair so that she had to observe her obvious disappointment
when she saw who her tutor was.

The time came for the walk and they bundled up for the
chilly weather. But they had barely turned into the little country
lane before the scientist was telling Dawn an unexpected story.
Beginning to cry, she admitted that she hadn't been out of her
room at Nottingham University for over six months. Dawn was
the first person she had told this to, and no one else in the city
knew her well enough to have noticed. Dawn was compassionate
rather than relieved at this unforeseen turn, but she smiled as
she told me of what she termed 'God's gentle preparation' for
this moment. She had recently read every book in our library
and listened to every lecture in our archives on the subject of
depression, and she was able to get this woman's visit off to a
good start.

I was one of the first workers at L'Abri who never knew Francis
Schaeffer. I hear that back during the very busy years of his

life, when many, many people made the trek up into the hills to L'Abri in the little Swiss cow town of Huémoz, he couldn't spend enormous amounts of time with every visitor but he did try to have at least one private conversation with each one. For the most part, however, they had to be satisfied with the chance to encounter him in a group. I'm not completely clear on this— I wasn't there—but everyone who speaks of him mentions the attention he gave to what you were saying and his obvious compassion for you.

Once a year, the Members of L'Abri, our governing body, gather from around the world for a week of prayer, business and reflection on what is going on among us. Recently we have discussed our method of tutoring and I was intrigued to hear that everyone, at all the branches on all four continents where we are represented, was experiencing a similar trend (though I don't want to overstate this, because there are always exceptions—exceptional terms and exceptional individuals). There has been a noticeable change in the interests of our students, who now seem less stimulated by our lunchtime conversations and by the ideas in our lectures. Of course, on both counts this might be the fault of the present crop of workers. Perhaps we are not as good as our predecessors at conversations or lectures. I am very willing to consider this possibility. However, even as interest in these things has declined, there has been an increase in the emphasis the students put on their tutorials. They want the opportunity to speak—and usually to speak about themselves. They want individual attention. They don't mind listening, but they want what we say to address their own circumstances, their own grievances. The context is more introspective.

This has had an effect on life at L'Abri, and it may be helpful to understand why it has come about. I have heard evangelical leaders in Britain say that L'Abri has 'gone psychological'. I don't think this is the case at all, but I can see why they might think so. Some people lament that the Protestant clergy is expected more and more to have skills in the two realms of management and therapy, and both of these can seem distant from the apostolic work of proclaiming the message of the death, resurrection and second coming of the Messiah. The truth, however, is that our culture has gone psychological. Theological ideas have always aroused human emotions, but today emotions are seen as criteria by which the truth claims of theology can be judged.

I have also heard friends who are genuinely involved in psychology say that they have seen people receive deeper and more substantial psychological healing at L'Abri than in other, and much more professional, settings designed for that purpose. We do not mean to act as counsellors, and in fact none of us at present at English L'Abri is qualified to do so; and we point this out to the people who visit us, though we are willing to listen to the stories they want to tell us. The principal reason we are seeing this change, therefore, may be that that is where society is today, but we may also be 'suffering for our success'.

Chryse and I spent our 25th wedding anniversary visiting Greece, the land of her ancestors. Our last night was on Patmos, the tiny island where the apostle John wrote his Apocalypse in exile. It was raining and we were waiting outside for the ferry that would take us back to the mainland when I looked up just as a rift in the clouds passed over our heads. And in that cleft I had a glimpse of a blood-red moon. Chryse saw it too and it startled us both, especially with all the associations it conjured up with the Book of Revelation. It was a full moon undergoing a total eclipse, and instead of watching the eclipse happen gradually we had seen it suddenly, complete.

In a lunar eclipse it is our own shadow that obscures the moon, and as I think about tutoring at L'Abri these days I feel that there is a shadow—our own generation's shadow—passing over Christian doctrine and ideas. We hear complaints: the doctrines feel irrelevant, the answers they give do not fit my

questions, or meet my needs, or heal my pain. People say that
the old ideas can't be believed in our modern world. Not only
our science has moved on but our sociology, our psychology
and our ethics have too. People observe that the history of
Christian doctrine is tragic, a tale of division, hatred, intolerance
and cruelty. This can't be the story of our reconciliation to our
Creator and to one another.

The most common complaint from the Christian students
who visit L'Abri, however, boils down to something like this:
'I know everything about the Bible and its gospel, but I feel
nothing towards them.'

This is a powerful statement, and quite frightening if you are
being asked by someone to help them resolve this. The person
before you blandly claims to be a Christian but the story of Jesus'
sacrifice for their sake, the promise of eternal life, the forgiveness
of all their wickedness, conscious and unconscious, the love and
generosity of their Creator for them—these ideas, so large and
full of hope, elicit no gratitude or other feeling from them. They
are bored with salvation and at the same time they lack a sense
of meaning and purpose. They are tempted to go elsewhere, to
resort to something that makes them feel more alive: clubbing,
hallucinogens, a relationship with someone they can see, an
unfamiliar religion. They cut themselves. They have an eating
disorder. They shoplift for no reason they can easily explain.
They drop out of the best universities. They stop playing the
piano. They are grey and passionless. Often, such people were
home-schooled until old enough to go to a classic Christian
school. They have always gone to church. And their parents love
them and make sacrifices for them, and plead with them to go to
L'Abri because that helped them so much back in the 1970s.

It's frightening because they seem cut off from help. Telling
them the facts of God's love and the evidence of that love in
history makes no difference: more than likely they will reply that
they know all that but it doesn't make them feel anything at all.
Or you can tell them that feelings are not what matter: the facts

of the gospel are the issue. And they'll say that they thought they were supposed to feel love and gratitude to God—and you're forced to admit that they should. But they don't, they reply. Stalemate. Catch-22.

Perhaps they aren't really Christians, then—but question them about any doctrine and they will respond, without energy, that they suppose it's true enough. They can usually go through the Apostles' Creed and agree with what it says, but they are much more interested in what the non-Christians around the Manor have to say.

Probably no other situation has caused me more personal heartache. In some ways, this kind of apathy in a person of great potential grieves me even more than a tale of real, evil abuse (and, very sadly, that kind of story is certainly becoming more common). The apathy is a threat to me in a way the tale of abuse is not. Dietrich Bonhoeffer wrote his *Letters and Papers from Prison* while in the hands of the Gestapo and it is that deadly circumstance that makes it all the more devastating when he observes that 'folly is a more dangerous enemy to the good than is evil.' How could this possibly be? And yet I think I can agree.

The eclipse of doctrine is part of our larger distrust of ideas. A friend of mine who used to teach history at Oxford University told me of an odd experience in the classroom. He understands that many people consider history boring and irrelevant and he rather prides himself on being able to tell it excitingly; but on this particular occasion, as he approached a part of the story that should have gripped his audience, he sensed that he was losing their interest. The reason, he discovered, was that his students could no longer identify or empathize with the characters in the story, because they were willing to die for an idea. It was a revelation to these intelligent young people that in the past there had been people who were ready to have their lives taken rather than deny the truth of something that could be called an 'idea'— and that often the surrounding culture thought them noble for thinking so.

The eclipse of doctrine is seen also in the ironic distance so many of our students maintain from anything they can call an 'idea'. It is a symptom of cynicism, an unwillingness to commit to any ideology. The irony is that, amidst this apparent disinterest, people will insist in a lunchtime discussion or a conversation that 'to attack my ideas is to attack me'. They are passionless about the gospel but are full of emotions about the world and its pain and injustice. Often, beneath their bland subscription to the facts of the gospel they are angry at how God's justice and providence and power work themselves out in people's real lives. Why should their attractive non-Christian friend be in danger of God's wrath when they find so many Christians to be less vibrant and worthwhile people? Why does the church, with its claim to have a relationship with the Author of life, seem anaemic in comparison with people who find meaning without resorting to the hypothesis of a god at all? They have read the Bible, they say, but they do not find it as inspiring as the average action thriller or love story.

Churches and individuals react to these attitudes to ideas and doctrine. We can form new doctrines that don't feel old. Or, like the liberal theology that L'Abri interacted with in its early years, we can seek to discover the meanings behind the doctrines. Or, as people who visit L'Abri now do, we can abandon doctrine—a system of ideas considered true and important—altogether as the thing that unites us and replace it with something else—perhaps common experience, or a common longing. So much of the spirituality emerging today is appealing because it offers something new for us to unite around. Only when doctrine is marginalized, people suspect, will there be peace between Christians. Only when doctrine is marginalized can there be peace between religions. When something other than theological ideas is at the centre, there may even be peace between people who believe in a religion and those who believe in none.

Let me paint a scene that may show what this looks like. There is a conversation around a lunch table. The topic, brought up by a student, is homosexuality. Things get pretty heated, but this is simply a sign that the issue is important.

First, a Christian speaks up who does not yet share in the distrust of doctrine, and they argue against homosexual practice. Some of the reasons they give are based on biblical teaching, others perhaps are not.

Then someone else chips in, and asks the first speaker whether they have any gay friends. When they answer 'No', one can sense all the power and persuasiveness draining out of their arguments.

There is usually a third person at the table who says that they used to disagree with homosexuality and hold pretty much the same opinions, and for the same reasons, as the first speaker— until they made some close gay friends. After that, they changed their opinion.

The topic could just as easily be Buddhism. Someone explains why it is a false religion. A second speaker asks whether the first has any Buddhist friends. They hesitantly admit that they don't, and their arguments lose their force. And then a third speaker says that it was getting to know someone who was a Buddhist that changed their opinion.

Such experiences tell us many things, and one thing they show is that we are relational and our relationships affect what we think is right or wrong and what we think is true or false.

Let me demonstrate further the importance of relationships in today's religious discourse with the eclipse of doctrine. Again, I will use things I've heard around a lunch table. A young man had been largely silent in our discussions but one day he spoke at some length. I found his description of his plight very helpful. He began by accepting that true ideas about morals and spirituality might exist but said that in admitting this he wasn't saying much because we couldn't be certain about these ideas. We know that we can't be certain, he went on, because everyone disagrees about these things. If we could be certain, there would be agreement.

This is standard fare in a pluralistic environment, but it was when he proceeded further that I found he had much to teach me about how people currently think. He said that because we can't be certain about our ideas we become pragmatic. What is crucial about an idea, after all, is not whether it is true but whether it works. And for this fellow an idea's 'working' meant that it gave him meaning and brought him happiness.

He had linked these thoughts together. Because we can't be certain about our ideas and because we become pragmatic about meaning and happiness, we take refuge in relationships. If you can't be sure that you're right, don't place weight on ideas but get to know people instead. Ideas get in the way of relationships, because we can't agree with each other. 'When did an idea ever bring me happiness?' he asked. 'But friendships help me all the time to find meaning and happiness.' He shrugged, as I recall. 'Being wrong in your ideas is not such a bad thing. You get used to it.'

This quiet outburst made sense for me of so many things I had been seeing in the attitudes of those who believed the gospel in a way but felt nothing towards it. Relationships are more important than ideas to many of the people who come to L'Abri, and therefore they consider emotions more reliable than reason to get them what they want. And because today we prefer good relationships to right ideas, having the right ethos is more important than what we actually say.

Ethos is the tone or sentiment of a person or community. With the eclipse of doctrine, relationship replaces doctrine at the centre as the thing we unite around. Emotions can become the means to know what is best, and tone of voice is more crucial than the content of communication. We can be sure of our ethos—that is, we can control our tone of voice, even when we find we can't be sure about our doctrine. We can find agreement, and enhance relationships, in ethos (or tone of voice) even when we cannot find agreement in doctrine. Paying careful attention to getting the right tone is better for relationships than paying attention to getting the right ideas.

I have seen the consequences of this eclipse around me in England. The church that is interested in doctrine frequently has a tone that puts people off. A church that gives great emphasis to its tone often does so at a cost to its doctrine. No one should be able to say that God is angry with his world and its people with a tone free of emotion.

This is one reason why the tutorial has replaced the lecture— and even the public discussion—as the thing the students at L'Abri look forward to and benefit from most. It is not just a matter of L'Abri 'going psychological' or the affluent West being morosely introspective.

I disagree with much of what the young man said. I don't think it all hangs together as seamlessly as he thought—and yet I greatly respect his account of his inner world and his attempts to cope with his uncertainty in a society full of very diverse voices. L'Abri has always valued reason and thinking and ideas and doctrine; but I have a great sympathy for people who wish to emphasize ethos instead of doctrine. This is because when we focus on doctrine we act as if the goal of theology is knowledge and the key to right religion is thinking the right things. This is true after a fashion; but it is so incomplete and is such an abridgement of the Bible's teaching that it leads to the do-nothing and feel-nothing faith that we see in the students who visit us.

Success in theology is needed for success in life, and the goal of theology is wisdom, not knowledge. Wisdom is the integration of knowledge and emotion and behaviour with reality. So, in Christian theology wisdom is the integration of my intellect and my heart and my deliberate action in this universe with this Creator, this Fall, this curse of all things. It is also how I think and feel and act with this hope of redemption and the promise of the Kingdom of God.

These things make demands on our minds. The evangelical church, with its proper fear that people will try to save themselves by some self-righteousness, is very expert at asking people to make the proper demands on their minds. We are less expert at showing by example that these doctrines also make demands on our emotions. We have reason both to lament and to rejoice, because our doctrine reflects both the brokenness and the beauty of our existence. These things also make demands on our actions in the world. We are followers of Jesus. We are to live as such and not merely to think or feel as such.

The students at L'Abri want an integrated life and I'm glad they are no longer satisfied with knowledge alone. That is, unless it is knowledge of the Living God, a relationship that involves the whole person: heart, mind and will.

Ethos is more integrated than doctrine because, properly done, it attempts to integrate knowledge with emotions. Ethos recognizes that emotions must not be ignored in a quest for knowledge. But wisdom, too, is more integrated than knowledge. Ethos can be tempted to ignore knowledge, because you can say very different things in the same loving tone of voice. Wisdom is more whole than ethos because it demands that the doctrines we believe find expression in our behaviour.

In my conversations with the students at L'Abri I find that we don't need to change Christian doctrine but we do need to emphasize wisdom as the goal and not merely knowledge. Wisdom acts in its day and refuses to live in the past, and yet wisdom does not throw out the past as if it had no value. Wisdom is in no danger of 'going psychological' and becoming lost in interminable self-evaluation, but nor does it treat people as doctrine machines.

# How Doth the Old Black Book?

*"There is no use in evangelicalism seeming to get larger and larger, if at the same time appreciable parts of evangelicalism are getting soft at that which is the central core—namely, the Scriptures."*

Francis Schaeffer

L'Abri began at a time when a 'battle for the Bible' was raging. Schaeffer taught that the evangelical position (and by that he meant the true, orthodox doctrine through all of church history) was that the Bible was God's own revelation in every aspect and that all it taught was true and accurate. The two most prominent adversaries to the evangelical idea identified by Schaeffer were existential philosophy and neo-orthodox theology. At times, he even wrote of these two as a single stream, because of their convergent influence on one another and their similar effects on the life and thought of the church.[12] Both divided life and revelation into what he called a 'lower story' (the realm in which things can be verified or falsified as factual or not) and an 'upper story' (a realm that is fundamentally irrational and immune to the process of investigation).

The upper story was a place where religious opinions could hide from unfriendly scepticism. If religious faith in the Bible took refuge in the upper story, this meant that it could claim to speak religious truth without having to defend the Bible when it talked about matters of history or science. Schaeffer was adamant that this was a very grave mistake. He insisted that if

[12] This idea crops up in many places, but see especially *No Final Conflict*.

the Bible was untrue in the lower story, that place which our reason and method can explore, then there was no motive, other than a desire for personal comfort, to believe that it was reliable as a communicator of religious truth in the upper story.

People grow weary of battles; fatigue sets in and time moves on. What is the situation today as seen from L'Abri? I must say it that way because, although we have contact with many who are currently teaching or studying theology, L'Abri is not itself an academic institution.

There have been many changes in the past 50 years. There are the many movements whose names are a reference to what has come before—that is, all the 'posts'. There are both post-liberals and post-evangelicals. There is that shift in culture and in theories of knowledge called 'postmodernism'. The failure of historical criticism to feed the soul of the church has given rise to the reading technique of narrative theology. Also following this perceived failure, a highly philosophical movement called 'radical orthodoxy' is attempting to exclude from theology the techniques of the social sciences, which have often displaced those of the natural sciences in the study of the Bible.

And, as the surrounding culture has grown increasingly indifferent to Christianity, there have been stirrings among conservatives of ecumenism, something that during Schaeffer's career was primarily the province of his liberal adversaries.

There have been many changes, but there has also been great continuity. Fifty years ago there were four crucial aspects to a basic doctrine of scripture, I believe, and the same is true today: inspiration, authority, hermeneutics and canonicity.

The inspiration of the scriptures was the question that preoccupied the 'battle for the Bible'. It involved great struggles over many questions. In what sense could we claim that God was author of the scriptures of the Jews and the Christians? What role did the human authors play in their writing? How did the constraints of human language limit the Bible's message? It was really the question of divine revelation. Could a book with human authors and human language be a vehicle capable of carrying the weight of revelation? (This is to see it from the reader's perspective.)

We might also ask: Could the Creator God use such a human artefact, coming to us through the minds and pens of prophets and apostles, to reveal himself to his creation if he so desired? If one begins by answering this second question 'No', then the process of revelation is stopped before it even starts.

Some argued that the Bible was not inspired in this sense, that its power to carry the weight of revelation was very limited, that it only *became* revelation to a person due to an illuminating act of God's Spirit. But the Bible is God's revelation of himself whether it is accepted as such or not. It is true even if it goes unrecognized. It is not our reaction to the Bible that causes it to be revelation. In the same way, a traffic sign warns us accurately of the road conditions ahead even if we are distracted and pay it no attention. It fails to act on us as a warning, but the problem does not lie in the language or the skill of the sign-makers.

Schaeffer and L'Abri had a very particular place in the battle. One of the terms found over and over again in Schaeffer's books is 'propositional truth'. By this he meant that language itself could be used reliably and clearly to communicate. He did not deny the workings of language, but he did not allow that these complex and debatable workings turned language into a hopeless morass of non-communication. Even the most radical doubters of the capabilities of language will clear the lecture hall when someone at the back yells 'Fire!' in a tongue they understand.

And when one reads the Bible, especially if one can do so in the original Hebrew, Greek or Aramaic, it is obvious that its authors have wonderfully different personalities. The prophets, for example, could begin their prophecies, 'This is what the LORD says' and their words did accurately express the mind of God in human language; but they were not mere mediums who 'channelled' God's message without giving it any of their own character or perspective. But nor did they allow the turbulence of their own personal response to the acts or words of God they had witnessed or heard to distort that message. God revealed himself in mighty deeds, and the prophets knew how to interpret their meaning. Both God and his messengers were engaged in the process of inspiration.

L'Abri would not deny that the Holy Spirit of God opens eyes to real meanings and truth. (My own conversion was largely the result of reading the Gospel of Matthew in a single sitting and experiencing almost a physical sensation of scales falling from my eyes.) And yet the Bible's revelation is just as true if a person denies it, ignores it or never even encounters it. Our knowing of something can change our lives and our perspectives very deeply, but Pluto was orbiting the Sun and its gravity was influencing the course of our own planet long before its discovery in 1930. There is no reason to think otherwise. In the same way, a Bible resting unopened on a coffee table is still the revelation of God.

What does such an understanding of inspiration have to say, then, about the reliability of the Bible? Was it merely infallible in revealing those things 'necessary for our life and our salvation'? Schaeffer was clear that L'Abri believed in the 'inerrancy' of the Bible: the book was not only reliable when discussing invisible, spiritual aspects of human existence but could be trusted when it described the cosmos in ways that could be investigated. As it is expressed in statements of L'Abri's basic principles: 'Being wholly and verbally God-given, Scripture is without error or fault in all its teaching, no less in its statements about God's acts in creation, the natural world, ethics, world history, and its own literary origins under God, than in its witness to God's saving grace in individual lives.'

For Schaeffer's generation, if the Bible was inspired in such a way, then that was the source of its authority. Not everyone who was persuaded of its inspiration obeyed it, but they knew that they should. At the beginning of the 21st century, however, this straightforward relationship between inspiration and authority is not clear to everyone who visits L'Abri. For this reason, the battle over inspiration and the language it was framed in can seem dated to contemporary ears. The truth alone of the Bible is no longer considered an adequate reason to give its teachings a place of authority in people's thinking, emotions and behaviour. People rarely want to talk about the Bible's inspiration or the need for propositional truth, and yet any discussion of its authority will result in a highly charged conversation and heated disagreement.

If you have read the previous chapters carefully, you may already see something of why this might be. Words alone are now seen as largely irrelevant or impotent. Words alone—even true words—are suspected of being part of the problem of this world, not part of any solution. This deep-set suspicion is at least partially derived from contemporary philosophy. However, even people who have heard little of the philosophy have been affected by their experience of how words differ from reality. Just as G E Lessing maintained that an 'ugly great ditch' prevents us from arguing from the contingent facts of history to a universal and necessary ethic, so today's L'Abri students do not think one can argue from propositions that are true to warm relationships and satisfied emotions. Though, of course, in spite of their suspicion of words, they do acknowledge that some words are better than others: they consider stories more helpful than systems and other abstractions.

The problems with the Bible's authority, however, arise not only from our suspicion of words but also from a larger suspicion of authority itself. I might have expected to find this attitude in Kostroma, a provincial Russian city I visited in 2000. I knew I was supposed to speak to an English language class at a local linguistics university but what I wasn't prepared for was my subject. I was told on the 15-minute walk over to the campus that they were expecting me to speak for an hour and a half on the American healthcare system. I had no chance to prepare, as my tour guide talked for the entire walk about the history of the Romanov family, who originally came from Kostroma. However, by the time I left, the class thought I was an expert—they didn't know I was merely repeating the gist of an interview I had done two years previously with a former surgeon general.

Anyway, when in the course of the lecture I referred to 'the lessons of history', it was not a student but the teacher of the class who interrupted, almost yelling: 'History! Who can believe history? They keep changing the history!' I was not wholly surprised that a middle-aged Russian should doubt that she could know the truth, but the people I am writing about, with their struggles with authority of any kind, are the grown-up children of Western families, and usually Christian families. They have not been brought up in a totalitarian regime—unless the media are considered a regime.


Try this experiment some time. Do some word association with a group of people. As they breathe quietly with their eyes closed, say the word 'authority'. Allow them just a moment's reflection and then ask them to open their eyes. As they relate what they thought or saw or heard in their minds, you are, of course, actually learning only about them: you're learning nothing about authority itself. At L'Abri recently the answers have been dramatic: inequality, control of a large group by a small group, or of smart people by stupid people, or lack of control… These are just a few of the associations, but all involved a negative emotional response. People were suspicious about how an authority came by its power, and there was a perception that you had to be unworthy of possessing authority in order to get through the process of acquiring it. Most interestingly, people sometimes reflected that authority was OK if it was exercised in the context of a relationship—that is, it was more acceptable if it wasn't held by an institution that one couldn't talk to or influence. Outside a relationship, all authority was considered manipulative and coercive.

Lately in English L'Abri the students were so sensitive on this subject that they accused the staff of being on a power trip because it was always we who gave the lectures and led the seminars. They wanted to be able to give their own lectures. To show them that it wasn't strictly a power trip, we did let some students lead seminars, and this had some fascinating results— not least that they became more willing to listen to us. I bumped into one of these students some months after he left us, when I was surprised to see him at a L'Abri conference in America. We skived off one of the evening lectures and went to sit at a table outside a coffee shop. He told me with tears running down his face that our trusting him to lead a seminar on the effects of technology on our society had been a very important factor in his learning to trust God again. I could never have foreseen this result. That act of trust on our part had gone around his defences and gone beyond words.

The problem with the Bible is that (to use the terms these students use) it is viewed as an institution and therefore its authority is foreign, suspect, manipulative, coercive, uninvited and unwelcome.

The students want to be able to groan and lament to their authority. They want to be listened to. It isn't necessarily that they are rebellious (a mistake easily made). My colleague Andrew uses Psalm 89 as an example of how groaning and lamenting are allowed to the faithful believer:

> How long, O Lord? Will you hide yourself for ever?
>    How long will your wrath burn like fire?
> Remember how fleeting is my life.
>    For what futility you have created all men![13]

These groans are not the same as complaints or expressions of unbelief. In this world it is proper to hurt and cry just as surely

---

[13] Verses 46f

as it is appropriate to sing for joy. This example is found almost exactly in the centre of the Bible, and there are many such instances of emotional turmoil endured faithfully and expressed devoutly.

The authority of the Bible ought to flow from its inspiration, but in our culture people are used to deciding what they will recognize as authoritative in their lives. Authority seems to us to be something for us to give or withhold. And there are so many competing voices asking us to grant them that recognition. We deeply distrust any authority that exists outside a social contract in which we submit to it voluntarily. In fact, things have gone very much further, and our generation is very cynical even about democratically elected authorities. We think it immoral for anything to possess authority simply because of who it is—or simply because it exists. We think that a moral authority must deserve its power or else it is an oppression.

For someone today to acknowledge the Bible's authority it is not enough for us to win a battle over its inspiration. To persuade them of its inspiration and leave it there can be to do them a disservice because it leaves them even further from reconciliation with God. The inspiration of scripture is a vital concept: when the church makes concessions in this area, everything else soon begins to unravel. Nevertheless, it is the Bible's authority to speak, to command, to expect us to change, to reason and encourage and comfort—this is the issue that even transcends its inspiration. It is God's desire that the Bible should function, should perform, should bear fruit, not just exist. God's Spirit has accomplished inspiration even if the book remains unopened on the coffee table, but the Bible is meant to achieve more than this. We are not merely to be hearers of the word but doers. The difference between the two lies in the Bible's authority.

To help someone today to come under the authority of the Bible—there is a voluntary, conscious aspect of submission to it—it can be helpful to show them that the God it reveals does allow them emotional honesty, that they can lament and groan and voice their disappointments and frustrations, their sense of futility. Those who smile are not the only ones who submit to the Bible's authority. It is also helpful for them to take very seriously the Incarnation and specifically the attitude of the Messiah to his own authority and his use of it. The Living God who has all authority has emptied himself and become a servant as well as a master. This is the amazing process by which the Almighty God too earns and deserves his authority through his integrity rather than claiming it only by right as Creator.

If the Bible is inspired and if we come to recognize and live under its authority, it remains an intolerable situation if we cannot determine what the book *means*. This is the area of hermeneutics, the science of interpreting texts. Hermeneutics is now applied to every sort of text, but it began with the Bible at the time of the Reformation. That was no coincidence. It began not because people were despairing of the possibility of knowing what the scriptures taught but because they were intent on knowing it for themselves. With the Reformation, it no longer seemed sufficient for a Christian to rely on an authoritative Magisterium to do the interpreting and tell them what was meant. To settle for that was to give the authority of the revelation to the church.

Of course, Protestants do still believe in teachers who are responsible for what they teach and they can still subscribe to secondary standards and creeds and the early ecumenical councils; but it is the believer who has God's Spirit within them and the Bible in their hands, and who is in fellowship with others with that same Spirit and same word, who is best equipped to sit under the teaching of a learned and persuasive preacher. It always pains me when a parishioner comes to me after a sermon and disagrees with me, but I have to admit that they are not always wrong in what they show me from the text.

It is taken for granted by many who visit L'Abri today that Christianity cannot be true or persuasive, for if it was wouldn't

everyone be a Christian? In the same way, the presumption
is that the meaning of the Bible cannot be understood with
confidence or else there would not be so many competing
interpretations. Catholic friends use this same argument on me
to demonize the Reformation for its effect in fragmenting the
church into a myriad denominations.

The problems surrounding interpretation have not gone
away simply because we pay attention to hermeneutics.
Nietzsche expanded the issue beyond texts until everything
was interpretation—not that everything had to be interpreted
by someone but that everything we had access to was only
interpretation. Romantic art theories began saying that it
was not only the artist who made a piece of work and had the
freedom to create: the audience too must be free to create in its
interpretation(s). Remember Martin Creed, the winner of the
Turner Prize, who when asked about the meaning of his work
said, 'I think people can make of it what they like. I don't think
it is for me to explain it.' This is not a radical statement today.
This is standard and unremarkable fare. Given what we believe
about meaning and our inability to determine it, Creed could
say nothing else. But this is an 'every man for himself' of a very
different quality to that intended by the Reformation.

Postmodern thought has paid great attention not so much
to the activity of writing as to that of reading.[14] It isn't always a
comfortable experience to encounter this thinking, but some
of it has been very helpful. For example, at a L'Abri lecture it is
always interesting to ask students who bother to read the Bible
what it is they expect to find in it. This question, when answered
carefully, helps a reader to understand their 'pre-reading', the
mindset of expectations that accompanies them when they open
this book they believe to be inspired and authoritative. To know
our prejudgements and expectations is useful because they can

---

[14] A very helpful book on this subject is Kevin Vanhoozer's *Is There a
Meaning in This Text?* For an entertaining statement of the problems, see
the novel by Italo Calvino *If on a Winter's Night a Traveller.*

act as false boundaries and make it impossible for us to reach the author's intentions.

The same sort of dynamic is disclosed by the postmodernists' interest in culture and perspective. They take this too far, denying that there is a 'God's-eye perspective'. They also deny that if we make the effort we can get over the boundary that our culture or gender has put between us and the meaning of the scriptures. In fact, these postmodern theories have fulfilled themselves. For example, it was not long ago that a member of a jury believed that they were supposed to attempt to be objective, to step outside their race and socio-economic class. Perhaps they couldn't do this perfectly, or perhaps they didn't even try, but the culture and the legal system were in agreement that they should make an earnest attempt. Watch, for example, the final appeal of Gregory Peck's Atticus Finch in the film version of *To Kill a Mockingbird*. He is pleading with a jury of Southern white men to step outside their race's perspective and 'in God's name' do the right thing and find a black man innocent of raping a white woman.

More and more, however, we are told that any such attempt is doomed. After a big trial in America, jury members will talk in interviews as if they had been elected to be faithful representatives of the perspective of their gender or race or economic class rather than to make an attempt—however imperfect—at objectivity. If there is no God, this may be the highest morality we can expect: a faithful representation of one's cultural bias. The idea now is that if you spend time getting the right jury in statistical terms you will win your case. It is taken for granted that the experts can predict what someone will think is true from their cultural variables.

Given this interest in culture and its impact on interpretation, it was inevitable that we would begin paying attention to the same influences on the authors of the Bible, and so we have spent enormous effort on 'background studies' examining their cultures. We probably know more about first-

century Palestine today than anyone has since the second
century. And so the greatest question now facing a church that
still believes in the inspiration and authority of the Bible, and
still believes that faithful interpretation is possible, is: What
portions of the Bible are historically and culturally determined?
Especially on issues relating to feminism and homosexuality, the
church has to decide whether it thinks the prophets and apostles
spoke for all people for all time and in all cultures or whether
there are places where we derive principles from the text but
do not see the particulars as binding for us today. According to
Acts, the early church had to make similar judgements about
what we have come to call the Old Testament.

These are difficult times for the church in these matters. It would
cost us to change what we have traditionally believed. It would
also cost us to hold on to teachings that are no longer liked
or understood by our neighbours. But what postmodernism
should have taught us is that there is a popular, common-sense
theology, even on these issues, that belongs to our day and
culture. It is good to be suspicious of our own day's certainties
and common sense. We know that people today do not like to
pay any price for their opinions. The temptation to fit in to our
culture peaceably is very great. If I were to say candidly what
I think the Bible teaches about homosexuality, I might in the
not-too-distant future be prosecuted for hate-speech in the
European Union.

　　Schaeffer reminded us of another of Luther's observations.
'If I profess with the loudest voice and clearest exposition every
portion of the truth of God except precisely that little point
which the world and the Devil are at that moment attacking, I
am not confessing Christ, however boldly I may be professing
Christ. Where the battle rages, there the loyalty of the soldier is
proved, and to be steady on all the battle front besides is merely
flight and disgrace if he flinches at that point.' These words

are helpful: they encourage us not to shun the cost of dealing honestly with God's word, though they do not on their own tell us where the battles of our day are raging. But the point is not that we are to be people who love battles, who feel most alive when we are fighting. We are to be at peace with all people as best we can be. The real principle is that we are to fear God more than any circumstance or person.

Inspiration gives rise to authority. Inspiration and authority still require hermeneutics. These are clearly vital issues, but why an emphasis on canonicity? So few of us have a strong grasp of the process by which the 66 'books' of the Bible were chosen and woven into the one book of the Bible. This has always been an important topic, but today the idea of a canon is unpopular and under a suspicion very like that which hangs over the concept of authority. Western societies have come to question their own 'canon', by which they mean the accepted list of great books that have been influential and ought to remain so. Often this list is now critiqued as the work of dead white men, obsessed with 'kings and battles'. The very idea of a canon is considered wrongly manipulative—hasn't the process of inclusion and exclusion oppressed divergent speakers and silenced dissident voices that should have been heard?

This suspicion is echoed in our attitudes to the Bible. A recent student at L'Abri did not deny that the Bible was inspired, but she wanted to insist that Dostoevsky's *Crime and Punishment* was equally inspired. She did not want to deny that the Bible had authority, but she wanted to insist that there are other holy books in the world and that these too had authority in their cultures.

Suspicion of a canon, therefore, is linked to the suspicion of authority and cultural exclusivity. A good example of this is the film *Stigmata*. It was not a great film. It did not live up to the promise of its plot but allowed itself to be seduced away from the real drama into the 'spectacle' of grisly special effects. The real drama lay in the storyline, of the discovery of a new gospel which contained teachings by Jesus that were very embarrassing to the Catholic Church and so was suppressed. Scholars who knew about it were likely to be murdered. The film begins or ends (I forget which) with a black screen and a quotation from one of the actual gospels not included in the biblical canon. The implication is clear. How can we trust anyone to choose which books to include? They will use the criteria that suit their own interests.

The process of choosing the canon of the Bible by definition has to be separate from the process of authoring the Bible. Just because a book or an author claims inspiration or authority does not make the claim true. Catholics are more likely to invoke an inspired Church that could infallibly include or exclude candidates for the canon. Protestants do not reject this idea, but they articulate it as God overseeing the ordering of the canon with the same trustworthy power with which he directed the writing of the contents. The Reformers paid more attention to the reasonableness and reliability of the process as it can be studied historically. In other words, just as the contents of the Bible are not to be removed to an 'upper story' where they are spared the rigorous examinations of science and history, neither should the process of canonization be turned into an ahistorical mystery that we cannot question. This is one of the reasons why the Catholic and Protestant Bibles differ over the Apocrypha: the Reformers did not want to include in their canon of the Old Testament works not found in the Hebrew scriptures.

Learning about the process of canonization is not a 'vale of tears' where students lose their confidence. It was as messy as all church committee work can be, but I find that it stands up to investigation very well. Far fewer books were contested than most people seem to think. There were far fewer candidates that were excluded than most people suspect. And the church's attitude to many of the books that were excluded was not one of a threatened and hostile authority: often people were encouraged to read them for their edification, just not to treat them as reverently as something the church recognized as truly inspired and authoritative. I can encourage people to read the books of Dostoevsky or Augustine or Calvin for their edification, or the Didache, in much the same spirit.

I remember a time when I was asked a question after I'd given a lecture. A woman who was an astrophysicist at Cambridge asked me to compare the function of the Bible in a Christian's life with that of the scientific method. This was very profound, and I still recall the answer that I gave her—off the cuff, as I had never thought of the issue in quite those terms before. With a marker, I drew a large, pale circle on the white board behind me (for some reason, the markers at English L'Abri are almost invariably low on ink). This represented what I called 'the circle of all Bible knowledge'. We were concerned in this illustration, I said, not with the interior of the circle but with the line itself. It was like a big circular path.

If I know everything about the Bible, I have complete knowledge of it. (As I said this, I ran the marker again right round the circle.) This, of course, is not strictly possible. No one will ever have complete and perfect knowledge of anything, not even of something finite like the text of the Bible. This is not a problem peculiar to this book: it is a matter of the limitations of human beings in dealing with any book. Now, at first, I explained (and I began very slowly to retrace the circle counterclockwise from the top), one has no knowledge of the Bible. A reader approaches it in an *a posteriori* fashion—that is, they come to it to discover what it says and to find out if what it says is true. These questions of content and reliability are not decided beforehand.

As one reads the book, however—and here my marker stopped at about the nine o'clock position—one begins to find that what it says makes sense of the world. One starts to suspect that its contents are accurate. I said that I didn't know exactly where to put this point on the circle—it probably comes at different stages for different readers, and it certainly does not come only when one has acquired a quarter of all knowledge of the Bible. The important thing is that this suspicion that the Bible is true begins to grow long before one can claim anything approaching a comprehensive knowledge of it.

My marker resumed its slow movement. I was very nervous. I was trying to be honest, but I thought that my next point would be wholly unacceptable to this scientist. I thought I was about to admit to a lack of intellectual integrity.

The reader, I said, continues to read the Bible. Maybe they are also reading reports from archaeologists, maybe they have learned one or two of the biblical languages, but in any case their knowledge of the Bible and its message is growing. At some point, I said—and the marker stopped, not much further around the circle, maybe at about seven o'clock—they become convinced that the Bible is reliable. At this point, they start reading in an *a priori* fashion. This means that they approach the book confident that it is accurate and trustworthy. It means that when something is difficult to understand or hard to believe, they presume that the problem is with them and the limitations of their comprehension rather than with what the text is saying. And I pointed out that even this point is a very long way from being at the closure of the circle.

The marker continued its journey. At every point, I said, it is in principle possible that the reader will lose their confidence in the Bible and as they learn more will find that they no longer believe it to be true. But my experience is that greater knowledge of the Bible may also make it more difficult to be convinced that it isn't trustworthy. The marker stopped at six o'clock. It will take a lot more than one or two inexplicable passages or apparent contradictions to make me lose my confidence at this point.

I turned back to the astrophysicist, and she replied that this was, to her mind, precisely how the scientific method functioned. I had suspected as much but I had not been sure that she would agree.

I still think that this illustration of 'the circle of all Bible knowledge' is a useful way to think about the issue, and especially so when one is dealing with a modernist concept of knowledge. Yet I must confess that as I have reflected on my own experience of reading the Bible—which is at least slightly different from anyone else's—I find that the illustration can also be misleading. I was raised in a household that nominally believed that the Bible was true. I didn't come to it as a thoroughly objective reader as my illustration might imply. Many visitors to L'Abri have a background similar to mine and feel familiar with the book and its contents before they begin reading it seriously. Yet their reactions to that sense of familiarity differ. Some hold it against the Bible, feeling that it makes it less interesting or reliable. Others find that it prejudices them in its favour, making them more likely to trust its message as accurate.

I wasn't very interested in the scriptures until I had left behind the convictions I had been raised in. I went back to the Bible primarily because I was both attracted and repelled by relationships I had experienced with people who believed this book passionately. And when I read the Gospel of Matthew at a single sitting in a cabin in Colorado, I was convinced of its truth by the end of that afternoon. However, this process of conviction is not best expressed in terms of shifting from *a posteriori* to *a priori* reading. What had occurred was that I fell in love with the character of Jesus who I met in that short book.

Falling in love has elements of truth claims involved, but it far exceeds these. Falling in love is not a leap into an irrational state in which the loved one and one's emotional reactions to them cannot be discussed, analysed and understood. We are still dealing with what may be called 'propositional truth'. If we disagree with this, it is because we have accepted a kind of romantic philosophy that in the West contends that love is a passion that human beings suffer as witless victims. Falling in love, despite the testimony of popular music, does involve the intellect. However, it is a much more integrated thing than mere intellectual assent to the attractiveness of the other—even mathematicians appreciate the elegance of their theories and suspect that an 'ugly' equation is not true. Falling in love engages the mind and the emotions and the will and the actions. The idea of 'the circle of all Bible knowledge' suggests that the reader's interaction with the Bible is a matter that involves only the intellect.

My 'falling in love' had a content and it had its reasons. I appreciated the character of Jesus, I was amazed at his teachings, I admired his willingness to live according to his words. I was persuaded of his integrity and of his identity. I began to see that he was the fulfilment of the covenants and the prophecies. I was grateful for what he apparently did for me. I sensed in following him a reason to live and something worth doing. These are not 'upper story' matters, and yet being persuaded of these things demanded much more than Cartesian intellectual assent.

When people ask me to describe the function of the Bible in the Christian's life I still draw the circle, because our reason does contribute to our decisions, especially in any decision to continue to remain in love. But I also tell the story of that afternoon reading alone in the cabin and of that initial infatuation.

Atticus Finch appealed to a jury of Southern white men in a hot courtroom. I myself am a Southern white man, though of a different generation. The jury, however, found Finch's client guilty: they refused to rise above their vested cultural interests and prejudices. Because people do this in reality, I have to tell the second story of how my affections changed and I fell in love with the Christ. But because everyone in the film's audience—and, I suspect, most of the jurymen in the film, too—know the jury is making the wrong decision and feel the injustice of it deeply, because people do *this* in reality, I also continue to draw the circle on the board.

# Seeing the World and Standing Still

*"The person who escapes in alcohol and then acts shocked when his child uses drugs is being unreasonable."*

Francis Schaeffer

I came to England in 1992, not long ago really in the scheme of things; and yet there have been great changes since then. Back then, Greatham was a sleepy village, sleepy but with a lot of traffic flowing through it. The army camp down the road trained drivers for armoured personnel carriers, which clanked by in front of the Manor, billowing diesel smoke. Back then, when I needed library facilities to gather information for my lectures I found that English librarians were very protective of their collections. (When I visited Cambridge University, they took my camera from me and made me wear a yellow badge proclaiming that I was a visitor, and I had to be conducted around by a member of staff.) I was very aware that I was living in the countryside.

Today, Greatham remains a sleepy village. They have built a by-pass and introduced traffic-calming measures, so there is much less traffic now. The tracked vehicles with all the helmets sticking out of the hatches now go a different way. But the internet arrived in 1993 and today I can sit in my little office and access the world. It's no longer so obvious to me that I live in the countryside. I can find out things without negotiating with the library. This has been an improvement for me, I think.

The students at English L'Abri have their day off on Thursday. This is convenient for them because most of the places they may wish to visit are not as crowded then as on Saturdays, but it is our traditional schedule because we want to be open for British university students or other groups to visit on weekends. My years in this country have gone by quickly, but the use of free time has changed drastically from where I sit to observe it.

I love to go to breakfast over at the Manor on Thursday mornings. It is very relaxed. It is 30 minutes later than ordinarily, and one doesn't have to come down at all unless one wants to. I like to ask people how they plan to use their day, and then I live vicariously through their adventures. The English weather makes some days better for curling up in the living room by the fire and reading a thick book or having a conversation. But if one wants to be more active, there are cathedral cities to visit or footpaths through the Hangers, our local hills. You can walk up to Hawkley and have a warm pub lunch or go and see Jane Austen's house in Chawton. London, with its art galleries and museums and theatres, Parliament and the Palace, is just over an hour away by train. However, the great difference is that most students now decide that their first priority is to find somewhere with internet access and check their e-mails. It has really changed how they plan their day. It's not nearly as much vicarious fun as it once was.

I am not opposed to e-mail so long as I use it and it doesn't use me. Things got out of control once and so I went offline for some seven months. I was amused by the reaction to my decision. Half of those who talked to me about it treated me as if I was a folk hero like Johnny Appleseed or a courageous non-conformist like Mahatma Gandhi. These people would tell me that they wished they could do the same (sigh) but it was impossible. The other half, however, treated me as if I was being egotistical and wilfully inconveniencing everyone else in the world. A colleague from Southborough L'Abri called it my 'cyber-suicide'.

I remember the argument we had among ourselves at the Manor about buying a fax machine back in '92. Someone had offered us money for the purchase and still we were not sure we wanted one. I was in charge of bookings and reservations back then, and I wrote personally to each person who made an enquiry. I wrote with a pen, making an impression on white paper, and it was symbolic. I wanted everyone to be treated as an individual and I wanted them to be aware that there was a person on the other end of the correspondence. It took a lot of time. It wasn't always fun. I wrote away dutifully most Friday afternoons, and then the snails took the letters around the world at a speed I considered amazing.

The fax machine when we bought it proved to speed up the pace. Away with the pens and paper! People wanted to be answered the next day. The pace of the world had come to Greatham with an insistent tone of voice. Nowadays, of course, it is all done by e-mail. The turnaround is expected to be even faster than by fax. More people contact us, book a visit and never show up than we experienced before. We had to ask a secretary to begin doing the work for us. Our webmeister, a former student who lives in California, tells us that there are thousands of hits on our website each week and the average visit to the site is a very long three minutes. Organizations around the world would pay vast amounts to have such favourable statistics. And yet Michael the webmeister finds us lovingly uncooperative with his efforts to serve us and our potential audience.

I remember the first time a mobile phone went off during a lecture in the Manor. I did not mean to embarrass the owner, but I commented, 'That's never happened before.'

We live in a world of total access in real time. The students remain in more frequent contact with their families and friends back home. Isn't that a good thing? They visit the English countryside, or even London, much less than they once did. I wonder about the connections. My son Gordon bought his own phone two weeks ago. He could tell I was sad about it, but he could also see my resignation. (I've already grown to like calling him and finding out where he is.)

People bring their laptops to the Manor now, of course. Nothing wrong with that. Aren't these just small-on-the-outside-but-very-big-on-the-inside notebooks? They also play DVD movies. Not long ago, showing a film was a communal event of some importance. In my office there is still a strange little window opening onto the lecture room. It was put in so that we could show 16mm films and not have to listen to the clacking of the noisy old projector. Video, of course, did away with the heat and the noise and the splicing. Everyone used to come to the film shows; now students sometimes prefer not to.

We do show films at all the L'Abri branches. In many ways, these are the literature of our generation. But in England we try to show only one, good film a week and to discuss it and learn from it.

Once, while my wife and I were exiled to America and working at Covenant Seminary, we hosted a series of evenings when we hoped people would learn about contemporary culture from viewing contemporary films and the seminary asked me to give an interview on Christian radio about it. I was sure I was not the right person for this, but everyone else who was more sure-footed with the media was away from campus that day and so the responsibility fell to me. I felt a secret sense of doom at the prospect, but I also had a strong sense of duty.

At the appointed time on the day, the telephone rang in my office. It was an assistant on the programme getting me ready for the radio presenter, Penny, who, she said, would be on the line and on the air with me in 15 seconds. Penny had a big personality, affable and very suitable for AM radio. Her questions were sensible: I was hosting this big lecture series on film and so I must be some sort of an expert. We chatted for a bit before she embarked on the investigative journalist section of the interview.

'So, Dr Bradshaw, what did you think of...?' and she named
a recent film distributed by the Billy Graham Evangelistic
Association.

I had to admit that I hadn't seen the film, and I fear that my
hesitant tone may have betrayed the fact that I hadn't even heard
about it until that moment.

The temperature of the conversation dropped noticeably.
Penny obviously had her doubts about my piety, so she turned
to a safer topic. 'Well then, Dr Bradshaw...' (Was that a trace of
sarcasm I detected in her voice? Had she learned that I was only
a veterinary doctor? Was I going to be exposed as a fake?) 'Let
me ask you about a movie that we know you have seen...' I could
sense the catastrophe approaching with the certain timing of
a Swiss train. And then she said it: '*Titanic*.' One of only three
films ever to win 11 Academy Awards.

'Well, Penny,' I said, 'I have to admit that I haven't seen
*Titanic*.'

Not only was my piety in doubt, I obviously knew nothing
about movies at all. Penny could hear people all over St Louis
banging the tops of their radios or changing stations.

My son Ethan studies a martial art and he has learned that,
when possible, one uses the weight and energy of an adversary
against them. Not that Penny was my adversary, but nonetheless
I did salvage the moment by asking her, 'But what did you think
of the film, and how do you account for its wild popularity?' She
did a fine job of fielding the question.

I bring up this worst of radio interviews because it illustrates
the fact that people like people who want to know their opinion.
After this, Penny grew more comfortable with me, and she
began talking about a question her husband had asked her
recently. Why do we have to discuss films at all? Why can't we
just watch them and be entertained without all the intellectual
mumbo-jumbo?

There is, I think, a fallacy in the question 'Why can't we
just watch a movie for entertainment? Why do we have to

think about it?' The fallacy is to set understanding and analysis against entertainment. To understand something better usually increases enjoyment. Take it from me: I've tried to watch cricket without knowing the rules. Not every worthwhile film is made in English by any means, and so we do watch things in other languages sometimes—not in an élitist or pretentious way: it's just so good, for instance, to see what an Albanian film-maker makes of the history of the Balkans. I have had students walk out in disgust when they saw that the film for the evening was subtitled, but that attitude impoverishes them, I believe.

I offered these thoughts or something like them to Penny and her unseen audience. She was not thoroughly persuaded, but at least I had finally said something. She ended the interview with a simple enough—even predictable—question. 'Well, what do you like to watch, then? Can you recommend a good movie for us to rent and watch at home?' In my defence, I was by this time pretty rattled by the pace, the pressure, the embarrassment. For the life of me I couldn't think of a single movie—except for the one I had watched the night before with Chryse. It starred Gérard Depardieu and its title was in French, a language I read a tiny bit but can't pronounce.

Penny signed off with me. Not many people came from off-campus to hear the lectures (which were very worthwhile) and I haven't been invited on the radio since. I walked down the hill to the seminary's administrative building. Thankfully, all of the sure-footed people were out of the office or doubtless I would have been fired, because I actually stood up on the desk of the secretary for admissions, who had listened to the broadcast and was laughing as I entered. I stood on her desk, stamping my feet and proclaiming loudly, 'I do not do AM radio!'


People come to England and seem to work hard at trying to make the experience as much like wherever they came from as possible. This attitude, though rarely conscious, also seems impoverished to me. And it's a little strange, because these same people are the ones most likely to defend the rights of cultures to be different and to argue that we can't get to the truth because of the influences of culture on our perspective.

We at L'Abri are not necessarily against any of the new information technologies, but I did once ask a student to think about not using her mobile phone while with us. She was shocked and could not imagine why I would make such an incomprehensible request. My answer made no sense to her as I spoke about stepping out of total access for a while, slowing down and listening to other sounds for a change. Her face could not have been blanker if I had been speaking Nepali to her.

We have very few rules at L'Abri. We oppose legalism, and we want people with very diverse ideas about what is moral and what is not to come and live with us. The few rules we have are almost always the result of a hard-earned lesson: life together really only functions well when we do this or don't do that. The introductory material that we send prospective students therefore tries to convey this freedom. We try not to have a long list of all the machines and noise-making devices that can prevent people from getting to know each other, that keep them busy so that they don't get to know themselves, that can even be obstacles to hearing a message from the Living God or his creation. Didn't Blaise Pascal, that amazingly suggestive and enigmatic thinker, write that the source of all humankind's misfortune is that we don't know how to sit still in a room?

We have art evenings, and it is truly a thing of wonder to see someone learn to create rather than watch others do it for them. It is also a scary thing for us these days. We are amateurs but we have access to all that the professionals do—and yet (it seems to me incredible) it wasn't really all that long ago that there was only live music in the world. If you wanted music, someone had to make it, like dinner. We also have play readings—and I have seen some unexpected trends: it really does seem that the person who 'comes out of themselves' and 'steals the show' is someone who is easily overlooked in life because they are quiet or bashful in the everyday. We have talent evenings. I can never forget the Anglican ordinand down from Bristol unexpectedly moving the couch aside and breakdancing on the living-room floor.

In contemporary life there are not many opportunities to sing with others. Many of us have lost the desire to do so. We sing alone in the shower or in the car, or if it's in public the volume is usually turned up so loud that no one else can hear us. This too impoverishes us: music is ever more available but we are always in the audience. So, we try to have music evenings together. Of course, excellent music may come at a price. A trombonist from a German orchestra once wrote to say she wished to stay with us. We were excited about having her visit, hoping that this meant we would enjoy a concert or two. But she went on in her letter to explain that while she was away from the orchestra she would need to practise four hours a day. Her scales were audible all over the Manor, even though she played them in the basement.

And I like it when we have dances. I know that Christians can be very ambivalent about dancing and there can be good reason for this, but Christians do occupy bodies. There is an oldish set of tapes in our study room which are recordings of lectures that Hans Rookmaaker gave to the students of Westminster Seminary in Philadelphia.[15] I winced as I listened, though it was decades after the event, when a poor seminarian asked the art historian about nudity in art. I knew something of what would follow. Rookmaaker, who had difficulty understanding the attitude of American evangelicals to art, began pounding on something and insisting loudly, 'We are bodies! We are not nobodies!' I couldn't see him, of course, but I like to think that he was standing on top of a desk like I did after my radio débâcle.

---

[15] These lectures and those given at L'Abri can be found in volumes 3 & 6 of *The Complete Works of Hans Rookmaaker*, edited by Marleen Hengelaar-Rookmaaker and published by Piquant (2002/3).

The apostle Paul writes meaningfully about our horror of being without bodies.[16] Dancing can be a horrible thing. I have talked to students about how they use dance and drugs to try to leave the world of reality. Clubbing can be a kind of non-permanent erasure of themselves. But dancing at the Manor is really a joy. All ages participate together, and though it is about bodies and about rhythm, though it is about being male and female, it is not about sexuality. Ironically, our culture is comfortable about sex but not about being men and women.

Volleyball is a passion for some of us at the Manor. It isn't so much that we are competitive, because we try to play in such a way that anyone can join in; but we love it because when you play with someone you get to know them in a way that doesn't happen otherwise. And because it's fun to move around in these fantastic bodies we have been given. Even those bodies that are not beautiful or don't work very well are still quite amazing. Many times I have told a student something about themselves and they have been shocked by my apparent acumen. I break the spell, however, by saying, 'I know this because I've played volleyball with you.' With one student, I knew that some remarkable spiritual change had occurred, before we had a chance to talk about it, from the new abandon with which they chased after the ball, diving in order to make shots, diving even when they couldn't make the shot.

This is another area in which we surprise each other. Dawn has taken an interest in rugby—and not just watching England defeat Australia on the telly. No, she has started playing it on the back lawn, tearing up the grass I so carefully cultivated to look like the fellows' garden at St John's College, Cambridge. And Rüdiger shows an innate ability in any sport involving the use of spheres of any size or weight. He spent a year in a football[17] team in Germany and looked set for a career as a professional and so

16 2 Corinthians 5:1–10
17 Or soccer, for American readers

I would expect him to be talented in that department; but when a group of us went out ten-pin bowling,[18] though he had never rolled a bowling ball before, he had the effrontery to beat me in our second game.

As my body wears itself out, country walking has become my favourite pastime with visitors. I once took a man from an American theological seminary out of the Manor's grounds with the promise that I was going to show him the best thing about life in England. We went a few hundred metres down Church Lane and I stopped.

'Well?' he asked, seeing nothing special. Perhaps he had thought there was a Shakespearean theatre at the end of the road.

I pointed to a wooden sign, leaning at an angle and green with lichen. It pointed off through the stinging nettles and said simply: 'Footpath'. We can follow these signs over stiles and through pastures. We can walk through Lady Selbourne's apple orchards and all over the surrounding countryside.

English L'Abri actually began in Ealing, a very busy suburb of London. It is important to emphasize that what we do at L'Abri does not require immense tracts of land in lovely settings. But it is wonderful to get people out of their cities and away from the fumes. Out in the country the seasons are more noticeable, the animals are more visible, human work is more obviously co-operation and garbage doesn't seem quite so inevitable a part of the landscape.

Dawn took us walking on one of my favourite trails one autumn, but she took us under a full moon where I had only walked during the day. We startled the sheep in their pastures. The village of Liss twinkled rather feebly in the valley below. People need routines and patterns in their lives if they are to flourish, but they also need to escape from these at times and see things from a different altitude. Our eyes need to gaze at something further from them than a computer screen.

[18] Or just plain bowling to American readers

Walking, of course, is a marvellous way to get this new vision of things, albeit a joy that too few know; but it is too slow for our Edith. Being from the Netherlands, she much prefers to travel the countryside on her bicycle, but being from the Netherlands also means that she is not really used to hills. Hampshire is not as agreeably flat as the tulip fields reclaimed from the North Sea, and she comes home from her excursions red-faced and exhausted.

People can take home what they like of life here at L'Abri. God lives everywhere.

## Microphones and Coffee Cups

*"Bible-believing Christians should never have
the reaction designated by the term 'shocked'."*
Francis Schaeffer

There are many opportunities to encounter new ideas around
L'Abri during a week. There is one's own individual study,
of course, conversations with one's tutor and all the hours
sitting around the lunch tables together. There are also study
groups where one reads a book or watches a film or listens to
music with others. These, however, are only the most obvious
opportunities, and actually most of the learning is much less
predictable and formal: working together, playing together, a
moment by the sink after brushing one's teeth. Where L'Abri
looks comfortably like the kind of education most people have
experienced is during our lectures and seminars. At the English
branch we have three lectures a week, and the one on Friday
evening is held down the street in Greatham's village hall. It is
open to the public and often the speaker comes from outside
L'Abri. Dawn goes down early in the evening with some students
to set things up and to make the tea and lay out the dessert.

It is very difficult to guess how many will come on a Friday,
so we leave chairs stacked at the back in case we need more in a
hurry. The size of the audience seems to depend on the interest
generated by the title of the lecture, but that isn't always easy
to predict. We didn't foresee, for example, that 'Hip-hop: a
Theology Lesson' would prove as popular as it did.

Dawn no longer instructs people to set the chairs out in
rows. We changed the arrangement after an Irish stand-up

comic came one Friday evening. She was very nervous about lecturing on 'Christianity and comedy' or something like that, so instead we let her perform some of her material as she would normally do and then we attempted to interview her about it. She told us she was used to performing in less sterile venues and before less attentive audiences and asked if we could try to give the village hall more of the feel of a smoky nightclub for the evening. Dawn was resourceful and found lots of small tables behind a curtain and set them out with tea candles on them and chairs around them. We were very surprised at how this simple change affected the feel of the event: people hung about longer afterwards and engaged in more conversation with one another. Since that night we have kept the tables and the 'nightclub' feel.

We plan the Friday night lectures some time in advance, and so I was surprised one afternoon when my colleague Doug stopped me in the front hall of the Manor and asked whether I wanted a friend from our church to lecture instead of him the following week. This was just 10 or 12 days after the two passenger jets crashed into and destroyed the World Trade Center. The friend in question was standing next to Doug at the time and it put me in a difficult position: all the lecture schedules had been mailed out and I had no idea why Doug would want to make this unheard-of switch. 'What would you want to speak about?' I asked my friend courteously while at the same time dredging up the courage to deny this odd request.

'International terrorism, the history of Islamic violence and our response,' she answered in a very businesslike tone.

This only made things worse for me. It was a time of obsessive debate about the issue. Everyone in the public eye seemed to want to draw attention to themselves by proclaiming their opinion. What was needed was someone who had been thinking about this for longer than two weeks, someone who could see beyond the dust that still hung over New York. How could I ask a friend why I should let her use our microphone to present her own view?

I have to admit that I'd been going to church with this woman for quite some time but didn't really know much about her except that she was away a lot. In answer to my question, she explained that her firm had been in charge of the security for the Twin Towers until two weeks before the attack. Her particular responsibility was to be aware of threats arising in a large part of the developing world, including not a few Islamic countries. In other words, she actually was an expert and had been thinking about these things for quite some time. Months later, when someone tried to shoot down an El Al jet in Africa, she was able to tell me what kind of rockets were used and how much you had to pay for them in the back streets of Khartoum.

We made the switch, sent out a special mailing to announce the change and had a fascinating evening as a Christian spoke authoritatively about the situation. The village hall was packed, with people even sitting on the floor. My friend did an excellent job of seeing through the dust. Doug wanted to have her elected Prime Minister after her performance.

The history of L'Abri lectures is really rather remarkable, even if not all are as stunning as that particular one. After you have worked at L'Abri for a while and have listened to the questions of so many people, you begin to see patterns; and you can serve the church and other people by passing on your observations. Not everyone benefits from every lecture. I know that my own experience of the teachings of Francis Schaeffer was that I liked a little of it but found a great deal of it confusing and impenetrable. Later, however, as I gained more experience of the world and its challenges, I frequently saw that he had been saying something, that it was something important and that what he had been saying was exquisitely what was needed. I just hadn't yet been ready for it. He had been far ahead of me.

The study room at each of the branches of L'Abri is full of lectures based on such observation. Our commitment to the principle that Jesus Christ is Lord over all of life means that this material covers an enormous diversity of topics. There is analysis

of contemporary culture (by its nature, some of this material
doesn't age well and has to be replaced). There are serious
attempts to understand the arts and engage in real conversation
with the sciences (these, too, need replacing sometimes).
There is material on spirituality and on personal emotional
struggles. In the literature section, you can listen to lectures on
Shakespeare and Tolkien, T S Eliot and Gerard Manley Hopkins.
You can also hear discussions of writers less likely to be included
in the canon, such as William Gibson, the cyberpunk novelist,
and Paulo Coelho, the Brazilian New-Age 'warrior of light'.
The largest section is predictably devoted to the Bible and its
teachings.

If L'Abri or Schaeffer are going to be remembered at all in
the future, I believe it will be for the impact of some lectures he
did with Everett Koop, a doctor who would go on to serve as
President Reagan's surgeon general. These discussed abortion,
infanticide and euthanasia and were subsequently turned into
a film series called *Whatever Happened to the Human Race?*
My response to these had been mixed. Somehow I had made
it almost to the end of my undergraduate years without it ever
really occurring to me that abortion was a moral question or
that Christianity might have something to say about it, and
I was very troubled by what Koop and Schaeffer had to say.
On infanticide and euthanasia, however, I thought they were
taking a strange line and were probably guilty of irresponsible
scaremongering.

The Catholics had already long been talking about abortion
in their reflections on human reproduction, but Koop and
Schaeffer were the first American evangelicals to get the message
widely disseminated. Within a decade I was discovering that
euthanasia and infanticide too were real concerns. We hosted
a lecture series named after Schaeffer at Covenant Seminary
and I was amazed to find that I could get some very prestigious
people to come and speak. One lecturer was probably America's
most famous convert to Catholicism, who had been a well-

known Lutheran clergyman before 'going over to Rome'. When he came and spoke to us he said that he had come to pay a debt to Schaeffer, because it had been Schaeffer who awakened him to abortion as a moral question during his Protestant days. So, in my blindness I had been in good company.

Maybe some of the material in *Whatever Happened to the Human Race?* now seems dated or inadequate, but this is because it was often ranging ahead of events and predicting the future. It was not analysing things that were already occurring.

L'Abri thus has a rich heritage from its first 50 years. The goal, however, is to remain faithful rather than to maintain our popularity or influence. The happy truth is that many of the things that interested L'Abri in the past now interest many other people across the church. Many of Schaeffer's concerns have come to be shared more widely. This is a loss of distinctiveness for which we are grateful.

This was brought home to me recently when I was asked to speak at the C S Lewis Society at Oxford University. I was glad of the invitation but couldn't imagine what I might have to say that would interest the audience I expected. However, at the Manor we run a tiny bookstall in a cabinet under the main stairs, where we stock titles that our students often consult and may wish to purchase for themselves, and we had observed that whereas many of Schaeffer's works were becoming ever more difficult to obtain, most if not all of Lewis's remained in print and were much in demand. I decided to try to account for this divergence in popularity of what one book has called 'the two most influential Christian apologists of the 20th century'.

Such a comparison could easily have become a contest, casting me as the spoilsport advocate for the underdog, but nothing could have been further from my wish. The evening proved to be a very engaging affair—at least, I know that I enjoyed myself. The audience seemed to appreciate my analysis and they helped me in my understanding, for several of these people (as you can imagine) were truly knowledgeable about

Lewis. There were, I thought, several factors that made Lewis more timeless and enduring than Schaeffer. Some of these had to do with their work itself and some with changes in what preoccupies our society. These interest me primarily because the purpose of L'Abri is not to become timeless but to continue engaging in apologetics.

Lewis was a fine writer, of course, working out of a deep sense of the traditions of Western literature. Few authors, if any, have surpassed him in using fiction as a means to discuss theological issues. Fiction may date, but if it is done well its appeal can endure for a long time—and this is very true in our culture today. And Lewis managed to evade the trap of propagandizing into which fiction that promotes a worldview so often stumbles. (Although Philip Pullman has denied that his trilogy *His Dark Materials* was intended to be an antidote to the Narnia books, I believe he has used propagandizing fiction to attack some of Lewis's most lasting creations.) Schaeffer, on the other hand, though given to painting word pictures and providing very clear illustrations, was not an author of fiction.

A deeper difference between the two men lay in their attitudes to history. Lewis was an avowed academic and considered it some kind of virtue not to take a daily newspaper. He deliberately took a very long view of events and very rarely took anything that was recognisably a position on a contemporary question. Schaeffer, on the other hand, involved himself in the social and political debates of his day. This is bound to make Schaeffer seem more locked into his period, though he may still shine as an exemplar of how to work faithfully in one's own moment in history.

Also, my colleague Jeff Dryden has helped me to see that Schaeffer and Lewis differed in their approach to apologetics in a way that would affect their appeal over time. Schaeffer was much more given to cultural apologetics. That is, not only was he earnestly involved in the debates current in his day but he was also committed to being able to point out to people the outworkings of their culture's way of thinking in its music and films as much as in the writings of its philosophers and other intellectuals. Lewis was much more likely in his presentation of Christianity to focus on the individual and their experience of life in a small world of relationships and responsibilities. Lewis is therefore timeless and universal, for people will always have trouble with their mothers or struggle with moral intuitions and unmet desires—whereas Picasso or John Cage or Fellini may soon cease to be problematical as in time they either become acceptable to the middle classes or are forgotten by them.

Again, while Lewis did a fine job of advocating a 'mere' Christianity discernible in several different traditions, Schaeffer was persuaded of the value of the Protestant Reformation and believed that it was a disaster for society to turn away from its roots in it. In other words, he was attempting to argue people into a much smaller and more tightly circumscribed position. Today, this can make him sound narrow and party-spirited to some ears, and these are two things that the culture that has developed since the deaths of both men does not readily tolerate.

I don't know whether either man longed for timelessness. Both provided very useful service to the church as apologists. If I myself prefer Schaeffer's methods and commitments, I don't have to do so at the expense of my admiration for Lewis's accomplishments.

Professor Kevin Vanhoozer has said that religious questions in the past century have gone through some discernible changes. They once centred on matters of metaphysics—for example, the proofs of a God's existence. Then they shifted more to the boundaries of human abilities: for example, they asked how human beings can claim to know anything. The questions, however, didn't stay to sink in that quagmire,[19] but progressed— very intriguingly—from epistemology to ethics and what makes for a good and worthwhile life. The direction that this stream of

[19] This is how the Canadian philosopher Charles Taylor refers to many questions about epistemology.

questions took makes sense, and I think we have seen the same progression through the decades at L'Abri. People want to know what's going on around them. Are there monsters? Is there such a thing as a soul? Is the matter that we can sense all that exists? Is the universe eternal, or was there a starting-point? If there was, was it personal, or is consciousness really just a perception of complicated biological computing?

As we struggle with these questions, quite often we become sceptical about all the answers we try and so our attention turns to the methods we use in our enquiries and the nature and limits of our knowledge. We begin to ask questions about language, for example. People do this in their work assignments around L'Abri, and we have noticed that it is especially true of American students: when a task proves difficult, they come back asking whether there's a better way of doing the job. We begin to focus on our methods and tools.

After a time, we realize that language and knowledge are complex, though we find that we can use them from day to day with remarkable success despite not knowing precisely and completely how they operate. In the same way, most of us can digest our food without really knowing how the process works (and even a gastroenterologist would have to admit that they don't have anything like an exhaustive understanding). And so, after we tire of studying methods, we wish to move on. We want to talk pragmatically, not about digestion but about the delights of food and its proper uses and preparation, and perhaps even its fair distribution around the world. Our problem, we begin to suspect, is that we have become abstract and detached from the issues. We become interested in trying to learn what we are to do with our existence. We turn to what Kant called 'practical knowledge', which is concerned with morality and emotions.

People can still be interested in metaphysics, but it is rare in my experience at L'Abri that anyone asks for a proof of God's existence—though I think it may have been very different in the past. Most students assume that I can't provide such a proof, but they also recognize that this doesn't mean that they can rule God's existence out. Another way of saying this is that few of our students are thoroughgoing materialists and those public figures who are, such as Richard Dawkins, sound very archaic to most of them. A third way of saying much the same thing is that postmodernists will at times turn to modernist arguments for the reasons they think Christianity has been tried and found untenable in the past. They may use the old arguments but they want new answers. Although they use human reason as a tool to critique Christianity's account of reality, they doubt that human reason is going to produce the answers they feel they need.

Like the ICU nurse I mentioned in the first chapter, people can still be tormented by the uncertainty of all they know; but we can learn to have a workable confidence in our knowledge. Something like the 'critical realism' discussed by N T Wright in the first section of *The New Testament and the People of God* is a helpful resource (though in saying this I am not endorsing all of Wright's theological opinions). People can move beyond their queries about language and knowledge—which brings us to the present point in the cascade of questions we are struggling with.

I have already described the first great tension in the current questions: students are sceptical about reason, logic and the intellect and are more focused on what they call their 'emotions'. The use of what one 'feels' about something as a criterion for judging its truth is a part of the new interest in ethics and the good life. It is not enough to answer a question logically but leave the person's sense of moral outrage unanswered. People can be led to acknowledge that the God of the Bible is the true God, but this does not in itself cause them to love him. People want something they consider good and beautiful, not just true and correct.

Most of the questions about God that I hear are more moral indictments than expressions of disbelief. Something we have

observed at L'Abri is that there are two 'stories' going on today,
an old one and a new one. In the 'Old Story', a person who
wanted to be good would go to the church and the God of the
Bible. They had done, or been, wrong, but forgiveness was
available to them there. Of course, not everyone wanted to be
good: lots of people were not Christians, many couldn't stomach
the idea of going to church and many didn't want to stop having
their fun and turn to God. In other words, even when the Old
Story ruled the day, there was no golden Christian past.

However, Christians in the Old Story saw themselves as
occupying the moral high ground and calling everyone—not
necessarily out of self-righteousness or arrogance, but lovingly—
to leave the mire of sin and come up into the light of the Bible's
gospel. And in much of the West, non-Christians were in
agreement with the Old Story: if they wished to climb to the
moral high ground, they would go to the church and the God of
the Bible, for that was where goodness resided. In the Old Story,
people would complain about the hypocrisy of the church—in
other words, they would protest that while its message occupied
the moral high ground, its members did not.

For the most part, the evangelical church, it seems, continues
to tell itself and its neighbours the Old Story. It continues
faithfully to call people to leave the mire of sin and come into
the light available through God's forgiveness in Christ. However,
most of the surrounding society has moved on and now tells
a new story. This is one reason why so much public religious
discourse seems pointless and why so many conversations feel
bizarre and confusing to churchgoers, for in the 'New Story'
people have advanced beyond the ethical nature of the God of
the Bible. They think themselves morally superior to the God the
church proclaims. If they were to decide that they needed help
to be good they might look to spirituality for guidance but they
wouldn't look to the church or the God of the Bible. Why, they
ask themselves, would someone want to go down there, or back
there, in order to find a good ethical life?

The problem with Christians according to the New Story is not hypocrisy in the church but what it regards as the primitive nature of the God they worship. The church continues speaking as if it occupies the moral high ground, but our neighbours think we are calling them down to something they are already above, a god they are sure they have outgrown. Tellers of the New Story believe that an invitation to embrace biblical morality is a temptation to settle for something inferior and immoral.

The situation is not unlike the early years of Christianity. People gave up on paganism because they could sense that their Olympian gods were morally inferior. Read Ovid's *Metamorphoses*: it is primarily a series of tales in which gods change their forms in order to seduce humans. Ovid wrote in about AD1. And then this culture was introduced to the God of the Jews and Christians. So obviously morally superior to the denizens of Olympus, this God was good and exacting but willing to forgive. The virgin birth of Jesus of Nazareth was palpably different from anything Ovid had described.

The situation is not unlike the early years of Christianity, but now the god who may become extinct in the New Story is not Zeus but the God of the Bible: the God of Abraham, Isaac and Jacob, the Holy Trinity. This situation is well advanced in Europe, and it has progressed since the deaths of Lewis in 1963 and Schaeffer in 1984.

Here, then, is our serious confusion: we do not want our unbelieving friends and neighbours to violate their consciences, we want them to desire goodness and morality. We don't want them to settle for something they think is morally wrong and ugly; we actually want them to hate everything that is unjust and oppressive and cruel. But we find that our generation thinks that the Bible and its God are all of these evil things. The Christian believer occupies a difficult space, a place from which it is difficult to communicate. The pressure today is either to give up on a love of justice and human value or to abandon allegiance to God as he is depicted in the scriptures.

Think of the hot religious issues of our day, the points on which our culture really disagrees with evangelicals on the way to live a good life. The God of the Bible is seen as homophobic. (On the day I wrote that sentence, the Archbishop of Canterbury was conducting an emergency meeting of the prelates of the worldwide Anglican community on the ordination of a gay bishop in New Hampshire.) The God of the Bible is considered misogynistic. He is regarded as violent and cruel, as revealed by his acts in history. He is prejudiced and partial in his judgements, treating some people as more important than others.

An acquaintance of mine at Covenant Seminary wrote a book examining scripture's teachings about Hell. It is a good book and a service to the church—but, for those who tell the New Story, proving that the Bible actually teaches the old doctrine about condemnation and punishment only closes the discussion. These people, after hearing the conclusion of the book, then feel entitled to say that 'whoever God is, I now know that he can't be the God of the Bible. *I* wouldn't create such a place of destruction.' We in this culture wouldn't condemn someone for their religious opinions. We wouldn't condemn someone for their sexual practices, so long as everyone concerned was a consenting adult. The central doctrines of the Christian religion, which the Old Story recognized as beautiful, are now almost incomprehensible to people. The Cross of Jesus as the means of atonement has been called 'child abuse' by a theological student at one of my lunchtime discussions. God's desire for worship can sound egotistical to our generation, and beneath how a god should behave. I can tell you that the list goes on and on.

This raises the very discomforting point that it is not only those happy to be called non-Christians who tell the New Story. Many Christians secretly—or not so secretly—also suspect in their hearts that they are better than the God they claim to serve. This causes enormous tension for them. They are people of their day and have much the same moral intuitions as the rest of their society. They may condemn the old sins but they feel less and less confident of being able to answer the question about why the God of the Bible would have such primitive and apparently tyrannical opinions.

One solution to the tension is, of course, to make changes in the God of the Bible. The motive for this is to save Christianity from extinction by making it more acceptable. One such attempt has been made by Jack Spong, formerly bishop of Newark, New Jersey. The title of one of his books is *Why Christianity Must Change or Die* and in it he proposes that we must learn to retain the sense of transcendence but give up our insistence that God must be personal. This change, he writes, would go a long way towards making the church's God acceptable to our generation.

Much of the 'Openness of God' movement, to take another example, can be explained as an attempt to make the God of the Bible comprehensible to us emotionally. To be fair, those involved early on in the movement were trying to take the Bible's teachings seriously. They maintained that Christian doctrine had been influenced and infected by foreign notions stemming from Greek philosophy. However, the real appeal of the Openness position is that it makes God more like us emotionally and reveals him as a risk-taker.

How should we respond to the New Story? Doubtless the first step is to listen carefully and understand what is being said, listening even if we find it frightening or displeasing. We cannot insist that our partner in conversation recognize that we occupy the moral high ground before we begin the discussion. This means that we have to argue each complaint against God, making the Bible's position as clear as possible yet without being unfaithful to the revelation. We can struggle incarnationally to make the gospel and God's will comprehensible, but we cannot do everything else that others may require of us in order to be acceptable.

We can explain how God has our best interests in mind as well as his own when he gives us instructions about worship or

sexuality. We can show how he is acting in kindness in working
through a particular people and a particular death in history. We
can sometimes lead people to suspect that they really do want
a God who reacts to evil with anger. We do not have to invent
a new theology to suit the New Story but we most definitely do
need to explain things in such a way that they make reasonable
and moral sense today. It is no good simply making ourselves
comfortable in our failure to communicate by saying that we live
in 'a generation that will not tolerate sound doctrine'.

Besides taking each complaint one by one, however, I suspect
that there is also an underlying problem we need to address
that is the ground for all the others. We as a culture have a very
small idea of how great the disjunction is between the Creator
and a creature. The evangelical church is also losing some of
this distinction. In the 1960s, we rediscovered a sense of God's
immanence in the Jesus Movement. God had been distant
and transcendent, but we recovered a knowledge of his care
and involvement. In those days, we had difficulty speaking of
the Creator with passion, but Jesus aroused our interest. My
colleague Rüdiger is younger than me and is frequently able to
help me understand things that seemed beyond me, and it was
he who alerted me to a change in the way today's L'Abri students
think. People are now more willing to speak of God and are
irritated by talk of Jesus. As a child of the Sixties, this surprised
me. I would have expected people to feel anger or indifference
towards God as the transcendent Creator of everything and the
ground of all that is good. I would have expected that anyone
who wanted to feel that God was near us and loved us would
prefer to talk about Jesus, the small, visiting God. But today
students are often irritated by the character of Jesus and more
comfortable with that of the Father.

This change in attitudes is a puzzle to me, and it takes time
to see its pattern. I would have predicted that someone who
was more comfortable with God as Creator than with God as
Messiah would also have a very humble opinion of the rights and

privileges that went with being human and made in God's image. And yet today we insist passionately that our consciousness, our ability to think and feel, gives us inalienable rights as creatures before our Creator.

In a way that would have seemed ludicrous to our parents and blasphemous to our grandparents, we imagine ourselves equals of a sort with God. We acknowledge that he is more powerful than we are, but we also know that 'might does not make right' and that if his claims to moral primacy rest upon his power then he is a tyrant and does not deserve our gratitude and devotion. However, when the Bible goes to the ultimate source of God's authority in all of these moral areas in which we might disagree with him, it founds his claims upon the rights of a Creator. No one else shares this status with him: there is the category 'God' and there is the category 'non-God', and there was an absolute distinction between them until Christ took on humanity. This is one reason why the Bible's confident assertions of God's authority can seem suspect: they are claims that can be made only for God and for no one else.

As we consider these moral problems with the God of the Bible today, we can discuss each one using penultimate language and reasoning. However, when we try to examine the underlying problem that is the ground for all the others, we find that we need the ultimate language of the Bible: the Living Creator and the Mediator. The evangelical church must resist temptations to adapt and accommodate its doctrine to make it more acceptable—and yet it must recognize the challenge of the New Story if it wants the gospel to be understood.

# Curtains in the Goldfish Bowl

*"People search for 'reality' and often refuse to
accept what exists."*

Francis Schaeffer

When I travelled to Russia once to speak at the annual
conference of the Christian Student Movement there, I was
nervous and felt they had made a mistake inviting me. What did
I really know about the needs of Russian Christians or Russian
students? Initially I turned the invitation down, but then my
friend Olga Lukmonova came to England and, sitting on the
green couch in my living room, told me that none of my excuses
was adequate. I lost the argument and so I flew by Aeroflot to
St Petersburg, not really knowing what to expect. It was snowy
and cold when I arrived, which suited an imagination fed mostly
on Tolstoy and *Dr Zhivago*. The students were friendly and
not unlike university students elsewhere, but a question that
surprised me by its frequency and its tone of excitement was
'Are you really Fiona's father?'

At that time my daughter was six. She had made friends
with Olga when she lived with us, and Olga had spread the fame
not of me but of my little girl throughout the Christian Student
Movement of Russia. Fiona, of course, thought this a very funny
story—and that is how parenting can be.

The Bible is full of encouragement to be hospitable to people,
especially to the poor, to strangers and to those who cannot
repay you. This is why we fight to keep the Manor from feeling
like an institution, or a hostel or a school. When you stay there,
you are supposed to be joining in with our regular life and our

families. In a generation severely disappointed by the breakdown of reliable family relationships, getting to know Fiona may be a more profound experience for a student—and more used by God—than our lectures on cynicism, emotions and families. Remember, people distrust language and logic and find them inadequate: they want to see things and then decide if you have anything to say worth listening to. The thoroughness and depth of the suspicion are hard to exaggerate.

We had a family come and live with us for a spring. The father was a very busy and successful obstetrician from Colorado. He and his wife have six children, and so it was unusual for us and inconvenient for them and it cost them a great deal to be away from the practice for the three months they stayed with us. We were very touched when a year later they asked to come back during the summer, but this time as volunteer helpers. They told me several times how impressed they were during their student term by a simple incident. A new student we seem not to have expected arrived very late one night, and they observed how Dawn rose and welcomed the new person and fixed them something warm to drink, engaged them in conversation and found them a bed for the night. The obstetrician and his wife saw this act of unfeigned hospitality and it had a great impact on their own attitudes. Dawn was doing nothing unusual.

L'Abri, as I have said, began as a family inviting people in. That is its heritage, but it has changed somewhat. In the early years, a worker family had students living with it and sharing all its meals. Imagine trying to deal with a child crying because they can't face school that morning and there are several guests at the breakfast table watching the interaction. It would have been like reality television with a vengeance. There were no terms and no days when the shelter was closed to visitors. Today, students live in rooms together, a family has most of its meals alone and there are times when the students do have to leave. These changes are necessary for the workers, who require a bit of 'down-time', and it is also good for the students, because some visitors can become unhealthily dependent on their time away from their usual circumstances.

No book about L'Abri should dwell exclusively on Francis Schaeffer, because his wife, Edith, was just as important—and in some ways even more so—in leaving her stamp upon this international community. She wrote extensively from her experience of capturing beauty in the everyday jumble of hospitality in the life of a busy family in exotic Switzerland. I am not really qualified to talk about these things, though I benefit from them. It was Mrs Schaeffer who in her book *What is a Family?* offered a different metaphor in each chapter. Chapter 10 described a family as 'a door with hinges and a lock'.

We face many dangers in our open lives at L'Abri, but most of them are no different from those attending any other life of ministry in the church. We can be caught up in saving the world and actually be losing our families. Answering the needs of the world can bring us such a sense of achievement, whereas the home front is a routine that rarely gives any boost to the ambitious ego. Students at the Manor can be very demanding, but it is often good for them if we show them that we will not sacrifice the needs of our own family to appease their sense of urgency. Often that sense is rooted in a past in which someone else was gone from their lives, perhaps off saving the world or doing church work or boosting their ego. The apostle Paul is very clear on this: you should remain single if you want to be able to give yourself single-mindedly to the wishes of the Lord.

The door has hinges. It also has a lock. Usually people speak of a *balance* between the two. This, too, is a good image, but for those meetings in Russia I used a different picture: that of a dance. My thinking goes like this: In my years of studying science, my least favourite subject was something called 'quantitative analysis'. This required us to practise making precise measurements, getting as close to perfection as we could with the equipment available. We had to use balances to measure minute amounts of powder and the task was to get the pan with the weights into perfect equilibrium with the thing being measured. Then you had to hold your breath and make your reading. There must be no more movement. The slightest vibration was an irritating interruption. I still feel this way when people talk casually about a balance in the Christian life—in this case, between the door being open and being closed. If we allow this image to be our guide, I suspect that we may become rigid, spending just the right number of hours doing this and the same number of hours doing that. Form begins to supplant freedom because of the word picture we have chosen. Life is about finding the perfect equilibrium and then holding our breath.

The image of a dance, however, steers us in a very different direction. Don't think of dance in terms of what you might experience in the mosh pit at a U2 concert. Think of something more like the waltz at a ball in *War and Peace*. At any given moment you will seem unbalanced: most of your weight will be on one foot and you will be turning so that now you are in front of and now behind your partner. Look at a photograph with a shutter speed fast enough to stop the motion and you will not appear to be in a stable equilibrium. But look at a video and you and your partner may seem a single, graceful unit, a thing of real beauty. A family at L'Abri is engaged in a dance with the needs of the community. At times, it will seem that there is far too much emphasis on the door being open. At other times, the door may be frequently locked. The circumstances of couples, single people and children vary with their personalities, and they also vary quite dramatically over time. You may stop dancing for a while, but you continue breathing and you are not rigid.

I offered this picture to a group of Russian students who for the most part had been taught that Christians shouldn't dance. Here I was telling them that the Christian life is itself a dance. It made for an exciting discussion.

Pippin is a small, black terrier, a cross between a Lakeland mother and a Padderdale father (breeds named after two villages in the English Lake District where they take their terriers seriously). She is nothing special to look at. My children had been asking me to buy a dog but I had put them off for years. L'Abri is such a strange situation: even a dog would have to be the 'right' sort to fit in here. It may sound odd, but I even prayed about the right dog. I gave her to my wife for Christmas as a surprise.

I remember that one autumn we had a woman living with us who had spent several years working with refugees from the wars in the former Yugoslavia. She was teetering on real depression and had some difficulty fitting into our life here because the other students just could not empathize with all the suffering she had encountered. But she would sit in the wind under the big pine tree outside the Manor's kitchen and pet Pippin for a long time each day. It was very helpful to her in moving on to being with the other students. Pippin has had that effect on several people over the years.

A great surprise of my life has been how different my children are from one another. I am embarrassed to confess what I must have been expecting. I suppose I thought they would differ in the way that models of cars differ from year to year, but instead my children seem as different as helicopters and motorcycles, snowmobiles and windsurfing boards. They are powered by different fuels, function best on different terrains, cannot cope with differing situations. Some of them enjoy the flow of people through our lives, while others don't want to bother to get to know someone if they are going to be leaving soon like all the others who came before. I want to teach them hospitality, but they ought not to be forced into a life that is more open than they can bear.

As I talk now to students whose parents became Christians at L'Abri long ago, I do at times fear that we can make idols that cause our children suffering. As we react to the culture around us, to the disappointing childhood or wasted opportunities of our own lives, we can with the very best of motives desire something better for our own family. We can harbour expectations of perfection that can weary the actual people in our family. Wives can be needlessly hard on themselves because their homes are not as full of guests as they could be—and, when they *are* full, they can never manage to make everything look perfect. The heritage of L'Abri is daunting to many of our closest friends, but in fact we aim only for a welcoming atmosphere that still allows us to be the real and weak people that we are. Hospitality is not to be a pleasure for the guests and a rack for the hosts.

# The Supernatural Family

*"As we look at the church, even much of the evangelical church, what we see is tragic, for often the church is using entertainment or just plain busyness to attract non-Christians. This is a poverty. But it is an even greater poverty if we need these to hold people after they are Christians."*

Francis Schaeffer

Everyone was kind when I left Covenant Seminary in order to return to L'Abri after four years away and they wanted to give me a gift to remember them by. I smiled mischievously when they asked, because I knew just the thing. There was a photograph of Francis Schaeffer down in the archives of the library. A copy would be fine—I didn't need the original. The picture caught the man in a classic action pose, rather like those American football cards that used to show quarterbacks throwing, fullbacks running through tackles and linemen in a three-point stance. Schaeffer was wearing a very dapper, white, double-breasted suit and his short, dark hair was slicked back. He was standing at a pulpit, one hand held above his head in a powerful gesture, the other holding a large open Bible before him.

The image is very different from the one that most of us are familiar with. In the photo I requested he doesn't look like a philosopher, or someone who Europeans would take seriously. I didn't want the photo in order to be ironic. I wanted it to remind me that, before all things, Schaeffer was a churchman and that, before all things, L'Abri thinks of itself as a Christian mission.

L'Abri itself, as I have said, is not a church; but at various times
it has helped to start congregations when it seemed right
to do so in the circumstances. Schaeffer even began a small
denomination called the International Presbyterian Church.
Most Presbyterian denominations are confined by national
boundaries and he thought this a mistake. The hope was to
build a group of churches across Europe that were connected by
doctrine and ethos.

I have mentioned many serious problems that try our
generation, but the one that probably causes me the most
concern long-term is the attitude of our students to the Church
and to the idea of any church.

I visited a mega-church in America one Sunday. As I sat
in the second row in the giant sanctuary with the friend who
brought me, I felt the same excitement in the air as before a
big theatre production. I was told that this church had 35,000
members and that 17,000 of them would be in the service that
morning, with 8,000 staying for the gigantic Sunday school.
(Large churches face certain kinds of problems—but so do small
ones: there is no perfect size for a congregation that avoids every
difficulty in fostering reality in people's love for God and for one
another.)

A couple who knew my host came and sat beside me beneath
the bright lights. They were very friendly, rebutting one of the
first criticisms you hear of these very large churches—there
could be warmth between people even in such a crowd. Our
small-talk turned very quickly to their work, however, because
this husband and wife were a team. In the brief moments before
the service commenced, as a host of TV cameramen and sound
guys ran all their checks, they told me about opportunities to
sign on with the new telecommunications firm they represented.
The wife jotted down their e-mail addresses on the back of her
business card and gave it to me just as the massive pipe organ

began playing. It wasn't too bad as sales pitches go. I didn't mind. Evidently they liked what they did.

The service was entertaining (which is considered necessary by many in a post-literate society). Big music and perfect timing. A troupe of dancing children did a colourful Jamaican number high up on a balcony. There were gags—pretty good ones, too. There were two large screens onto which were projected advertisements for coming events and all the background support the pastor required. At one point in his sermon, he ran up some 40 steps leading to the top of the choir as an illustration—both of something in the text and of his own admirable fitness for his age. He said a lot of things about the second chapter of Philippians. His words were crafted to be relevant and easily remembered. When he used a theological word that his audience might not recognize, he did so humbly, with a winning sort of embarrassment. Lots of people joined the church that morning; several made professions of a new faith in Jesus.

Then we went to the Sunday school. It was in a large room, of course, very tastefully decorated—it reminded me of the decor of a fine law firm. The particular class to which I was taken was mostly for older people, but they chattered like parrots over their coffee and kolaches. Too much of the lesson time was eaten up by announcements, but it was a sign of how active the group was. There were people to pray for in hospital, missionary projects in Mexico and Brazil to raise money for, social events to publicize. There was a lot of laughter over the leader's inability to manage the sound system. I was announced as a visitor along with several others. The lesson was mostly a digression from the text perhaps, and there was a little too much about the leader's personal opinion of anti-Semitism and an argument he felt he had won that week with his Jehovah's Witness masseuse. However, the class appreciated what he had to say.

Afterwards, a woman came up to meet me. She knew my host and was very personable, but she came to the point very quickly: she wanted to fix a date with me that week when we could discuss the opportunities presented by the telecommunications firm she represented. She wasn't deterred by the fact that I lived in England—that made me even more attractive, she told me. England was 'really opening up as a market'. This was the same firm mentioned to me by the young couple I had met before the service. I congratulated her, saying that it was a very aggressive outfit, and I drew the business card from my pocket. She examined it carefully and her expression turned to one of ill-concealed distaste for her colleagues.

I broke off the conversation and left her with my host while I went to pick up the coffee cups left beneath the chairs. I reflected on what I had heard was the passage for the previous week's lesson, in which Jesus had cleansed the Temple courtyard because they had turned a house of prayer into a den of thieves. The story made more sense to me than ever before. The irony was huge. These people were not exactly thieves, but I doubt that those selling animals in the Temple were exactly thieves either.

Going out to the parking lot full of very expensive cars, we passed the church's restaurant, health club and bookstore. My host knew that all this was very grand by European standards and remarked to me, quoting the pastor, that 'everything they build has a hook in it.' I didn't talk about the sales pitches on the ride back to her house. She had witnessed them both and would know better than me if they were typical or not. But I did reflect on the thought that it was from such churches that many of our L'Abri students came. They had reasons for their dissatisfactions and disappointments. There were many reasons why people went to church and many agendas, not all of them transparent.

Several years previously in England I had tutored a member of this successful church's staff, a youth pastor. I remembered that something had bothered me as I listened to him. I asked him—not as a trap but in an attempt to get at the source of my unease—why a teenager from the affluent area around his church should become a Christian. He began his answer by saying that not everyone who is wealthy is happy, that personal integration and fulfilment are matters of spirituality. He was quite eloquent and convincing.

I pointed out to him that some non-Christians would claim to be happy and integrated, to feel no sense of incompleteness or lack of fulfilment. He replied that they might say that but he doubted that it was so. My question obviously troubled him, however. And then, perhaps not as gently as I should have, I pointed out that at no point in his answer had he insisted that a person might need to become a Christian believer because the gospel was true, regardless of whether or not they sensed there was something missing in their lives. To his great credit, this young man sank back into the armchair in my office with a look on his face like a bombed building. He realized immediately that this observation was accurate and revealed a great deal about what went on in his ministry. For him, the gospel of Jesus was an offer of a better psychological technology—in fact, the best available.

If you have been reading this book carefully, you may see that much that the youth pastor taught is important today. The message of Jesus is not merely an abstract, mental truth-claim. It is right for our generation to demand that it should make some immediate practical, tangible difference in a person's life. Wouldn't knowing God produce something good right now? And he was correct that Christianity is not a disinterested religion: it offers promises of fulfilment that are embarrassingly sensual. If not quite the picture painted by Islamic theology of virgins caring for every need of the blessed in Heaven, still Christianity teaches that the future is going to be good in ways we can recognize as good now. It is not just about something spiritual and disembodied and wholly foreign. It is, therefore, right that a person should believe in the message of the Bible because they have a sense of personal need, because they have lost confidence in their own ability to manufacture meaning and purpose. This is so true of Christianity that in the 19th century the theory took root that the religion had been specifically designed by people to fulfil them and allay their fears of insignificance. Nonetheless, despite being correct in some ways, the message the youth pastor presented was seriously abbreviated.

Victor Frankl was the psychiatrist who developed what he called 'logotherapy'. He was a survivor of the Holocaust and it was his observations in the death camp that gave birth to his school of psychology. He noticed that the major difference between those who survived the camp and those who did not was that the former were able to maintain a sense of hope in spite of their desperate surroundings. That is, they were able to imagine a good future and this gave them the power to survive a hideous present. One prisoner might promise himself that when he was released he would find that girl he should have married and this time he would do it. He seemed able to smell her hair, and in the smelling he found a way to live. Another prisoner might promise himself that when he finally got out of the camp he would go back to Dresden and take over his grandfather's watch-repair shop and turn it into a successful business. He could almost see the crisp sign hanging over the well-swept pavement, and in the seeing he found a way to live.

Frankl perceived that those imagined futures were enough to keep these people alive while others, who could see and smell only the camp around them, lost hope and succumbed to despair. I cannot judge whether Frankl was right in what he made of his observations. What is interesting, however, is that it did not matter which good future was imagined: a watch-repair shop was as good as a lover for the purpose of survival. It also didn't matter whether or not that future could be realized. Perhaps the woman had died in another camp; maybe the shop in Dresden had been reduced to ashes by Allied incendiaries. It didn't matter so long as the prisoners didn't know and could still hope in their imagined futures. These worked psychologically even if they were impossible.

The youth pastor's message was far too much like Frankl's logotherapy, offering a hope that worked for you and made survival possible. The Bible, however, speaks very differently. In Hebrews, it talks intriguingly of 'a better hope'.[20] Its authors insist that it matters whether or not what one believes in is true. It matters (as the most obvious example) whether or not Christ rose from the dead as reported. To believe that he rose would be enough to satisfy the needs of logotherapy. The resurrection of the dead could be added to lovers and watch-repair shops as a good future that helps those who believe in it to cope with the present. But the gospel is a better hope than that. The definition of a better hope is that it works emotionally in the present but when the present gives way to the future it also turns out to be true. The gospel is not merely an intellectual truth-claim, but it is at least that. In our reaction against a message of salvation that remains only words, we must not fall off the other side of Luther's horse and reduce the gospel to a useful self-deception.

The youth pastor's message erred in another way, too: it promised too much for the present. We groan now because of the bondage of all things to decay. The whole creation groans with us, awaiting the revealing of the children of God. And the Holy Spirit groans with us and for us now, especially when we do not know what we should long for in the confusion around us. Because, though our world is wonderful and full of God's glory, in a sense it is also just an enormous death camp. Everything is in the process of passing away. We need a hope to get us through the camp. We need a hope that also turns out in the end to be true and not just wishful thinking. The gospel must be about something far deeper than what Schaeffer would call 'personal peace and affluence'.

Please believe that I am not being cynical, or even critical of mega-churches. Once in England when I gave a public lecture on

[20] Hebrews 7:19

the church growth movement in America, the room was filled,
and filled largely by pastors: British pastors hoping that a North
American could tell them how to pack their empty churches
once again so that people could hear the message of Jesus and
worship him. It is not enough to find fault with the Church. If we
stop there, we will not accomplish much of value. We must love
the Church, for it is the supernatural family and the beloved of
God. And, as with all families, its life is messy. If we criticize the
Church, our criticisms must be based in love and a willingness
to participate and work hard for her improvement. They should
not be motivated by personal disappointment, or an attempt
to distance ourselves from the pain of working on our family
relationships.

On the same trip to the East Coast on which I visited the mega-
church, I stopped by to see an old friend from university. I was
very surprised to find that her husband of 15 years was leaving
her and their children. The issues were doubtless many—and I
only heard her perspective—but they seemed to be a cocktail
of mid-life and money troubles. Her husband was a counsellor
at their church. This was a private tragedy, but again I thought
of the almost universal distrust of what is called 'organized
religion' by the students at L'Abri. It is not just the old chestnut
of 'the hypocrites in the church' that irritates them—it has gone
far beyond that. If one of the major engines powering disbelief
in the Christian message today is disappointment in broken
relationships, the church appears to them to have no answer.
Even those trained in counselling seem no different. They have
the words but, apparently, no power.

All of us, of course, are hypocrites after a fashion. None of
us can cast stones because our words of condemnation can be
turned against us and our own wilful evil. Our problem, once
again, is seen not to be ignorance of the truth but a failure to live
it out.

The first question the church council or the board of elders or the vestry should ask itself about a new idea or programme is not 'Is this relevant?' That is a good question, and what we do should be relevant. But if that is the first question we ask of an idea we shall find ourselves chasing fads through the forest.

A pastor who I worked under once in a new church wanted to ask this question first in nearly every situation. Was this innovation making us relevant to people and their perceived needs? He used as his gauge the TV show *Miami Vice:* its pace, its colours, its sense of fashion and sense of humour. This, he judged, would help to keep us relevant. The church's logo must not use an old font, just as its music and language must be contemporary and chic. The Reformers translated the Bible into everyday language, and he merely wanted to do the same to the Reformers. Now that *Miami Vice* itself is dated and out of fashion, he would simply move on to whatever is hot at the moment.

On first consideration this seems a good idea—though it is very easy to make it sound like a bad one in the safety of the printed page and without the responsibility to make real decisions for a real group of Christians. It would seem that relevance is what a dissatisfied generation is seeking. We often use the word like an indictment. Nevertheless, the first question we ask should be 'Does this new idea or programme foster reality in our love for God and for one another?' Our generation uses the word 'irrelevant' because it isn't careful with its words. What it actually means is 'unreal'. The church seems to lack reality, and people are entirely correct in insisting that its members must exhibit reality in their love for God and for one another. Instead, the church as known to many of us seems to operate on the normal psychology and sociology and economics of everything else. When non-Christians perceive that the Living God is among us and that we love him and one another, they will be forgiving of our choice of methods and the interior design of our buildings.

In that same, 'relevant' church, we met on Sunday evenings in two house groups. The pastor ran one in the north of the city and I was in charge of the one in the south. Over time, his group dwindled away, and some members even began sneaking down to mine. He came to visit us and see what we were doing that might account for our 'success'. The difference was really only which question we asked first. We didn't do anything that was especially attractive or relevant. We emphasized loving one another and spent as much time as we could getting to know each other. We sang—none too well, but we meant it. And, rather than new material, we discussed that morning's sermon and what we might do to practise its teachings. That is, we wanted to move on beyond words, to turn them into something tangible.

The pastor was a good man and very well-intentioned, but he was horrified by what he saw in the southern group. He feared that discussion of his sermons might easily encourage criticism of him and his work and spread dissatisfaction, and so he forbade it. I can sympathize with him. Abscesses of discontent can fester in churches and cause real harm. He didn't trust me not to let this happen, and for that we paid a tremendous price in a loss of reality. The implication was that the message we heard in the morning was to remain safely in the past and not to trouble us in any real way.

Dick Keyes, my colleague in Southborough, has taught me that cynicism is the ability to look through anything and see what lies beneath it. I read in a book on postmodernism that David Lynch's *Blue Velvet* was the archetypal postmodern film, which made me want to see it. It begins with a brilliant scene from 1950s America. All is safe and in slow motion. The fireman waves as his engine goes by, but they are obviously not going to a fire. The overweight crossing warden ushers a group of children across the road. Violence is found only on the television, and you can watch it safely while sipping your morning tea. The suburban houses have neat picket fences and all have the same immaculate green lawns.

But something happens to a man who is watering one of these lawns. There is a kink in his hose, and as he pulls on it to free it he has a painful spasm that makes him collapse. The audience chuckles as the man's little dog bites at the water still spraying from the nozzle, but the laughter stops when the film slows down and the jaws of the little dog now look threatening. The camera zooms in on the stricken man—we can't yet be sure how severe his injury is. It zooms in further, past the man and into the lush green grass, and continues its descent into the darkness beneath it. A strange sound begins to grow louder, and then we can see what is making it: the endless thrashing and biting of a countless host of beetles. They are forever at battle, devouring one another just beneath the surface of all those perfectly maintained lawns.

Lynch's opening is a great picture of the mind of the cynic. The strong belief of the cynic is that just beneath the surface of everything, even of things that appear good, is the real world. Beneath every relationship or institution is a hidden agenda of selfishness and meaninglessness. Marriage, democracy, capitalism, education—many of the people who visit L'Abri 'see through' them all to the power struggle that underlies them. Nietzsche declared that knowledge is power: in other words, when you know something, you can use it to gain advantage in this eternal war. Foucault went one better and said that power is knowledge. That is, whoever has power can decide what constitutes knowledge—what the culture and the age think is true.

The church, in America or elsewhere, may appear to be a green and thriving lawn but our cynical generation trusts in no institution or authority. The church must have a real agenda, the cynic suspects, which is actually only about preventing its members' kids from being naughty and taking drugs and breaking their parents' hearts or bank accounts. It must be about keeping women in their place—servants to please their men. But it also oppresses men, setting boundaries on their behaviour to keep them safe from each other. Otherwise there will be mayhem and only a few guys will get ahead. Maybe the church is a good place to meet people and do deals on telecommunication opportunities.

The behaviour of the church is easily interpreted by the cynics to fit their vision of the world. When you speak with them, it sounds very plausible. They are not fooled by a stated message of love and sacrifice: they can hear the beetles beneath the surface. This is a mentality that is very difficult to overcome with words alone. It's a mentality one finds increasingly even among people who will allow you to call them Christians. Using more advanced audiovisuals and setting the worship music to a more 'relevant' beat are not going to answer this widespread interpretation. Such strategies can, in fact, merely feed the beast of cynicism.

Jesus overcame the cynics, but only by dying a servant's death. He has told us to take up our crosses and follow him. The Messiah did not use the language of self-fulfilment. He did, however, tell us that in losing our lives for his sake we would find them.[21]

---

[21] Matthew 10:39

# In the Rear-View Mirror

*"So the Christian must resist the spirit of the world in the form it takes in his own generation."*
Francis Schaeffer

People come to L'Abri hoping to change in some way. But if they learn to trust the God of the Bible, to obey his will and to be grateful for his gifts—that is, if the best changes start to take place in them—they still have to leave some time. They leave to find their future, but they are also returning to their past. While they were studying at L'Abri, their boss or their professor or their father or their pastor or their girlfriend was not there with them to watch the process of change; and when they get back to where they came from, the changes are not always welcomed or understood. What was valued by people at the Manor, or any of the other branches of L'Abri, may seem otherworldly and unrealistic in their usual habitat. The responsibilities of their routine life flood back in. The media are there, clamouring for their limited time and concentration. Old friends do not see the need to break their old habits. Their family communicates as it always has. The church's imperfections have not disappeared. Perhaps in the shelter of a Christian community the tender shoots of belief and change broke ground, but what is going to happen to this tiny seedling now?

Someone once described Dostoevsky as 'the nastiest Christian you could hope to meet'. I'm not sure what this meant in his case, but the phrase stuck with me and I approve of it. A person returning to their past in order to find their future would do well to become a nasty Christian. For too many of us, that epithet may sound incongruous and out of tune. Far too often we think that being a Christian is going to make us nice. But the seedling is weak and at risk. It can trust to God's protection, but it has to learn to be nasty. That means refusing to go back to the old habits even if this hurts the feelings of someone you love. It means refusing to live by the accepted conventions even if this makes you misunderstood. It means being very fierce and uncooperative with evil, even when evil is dressed up as 'the way we have always done things here'. In more conventional biblical language, it means fearing God.

Nice people are compliant. Recently at lunch a Korean student was talking about how she and her mother were visited by a door-to-door salesman selling children's books. They didn't want any books, but their culture made it hard for them to get rid of him. They were nice Korean Christians. They sent all the right messages—we don't want the books, it is time for you to go—but they sent them in a socially conventional way. The salesman, of course, was not nice: he picked up the messages but pretended not to understand them. He stayed in their home for six hours. The student said that now, as a result of this incident, she never pays even the slightest attention to any salesman, even if they may be selling something she needs. She doesn't wait to find out.

I would say that even now she is still being nice. For this Korean, becoming nasty would mean that she could open the door and listen to someone until she had made up her mind and then she could either make a purchase or send them packing. If this sounds selfish to you, I would put it to you that it is actually the more loving way to live. Being nice is not the same as loving oneself or loving God or loving one's neighbour. Instead, the fruit of the Spirit is love, joy, peace, patience, kindness, goodness, faithfulness, gentleness and self-control. These are a portrait of the Messiah—and no one who dealt with him ever accused him of being nice. It was in this way that he came bringing not peace but a sword.[22]

The apostle Paul teaches that we will all serve someone, whether we serve the flesh or serve the Spirit.[23] In much the same way, it seems that we will all fear someone or something. We may fear others or our circumstances or the future or God. We can choose who we serve and in much the same way I think we can choose who or what we fear.[24] What it seems we cannot choose is a life without fear. The person who looks most fearless to other people is the person who has chosen to fear God and God alone. This is why martyrs and holy people rather frighten us: we can sense that they have given up on being nice and have become nasty. They are no longer playing by the usual rules.

Nasty Christians, however, are not selfish. They want you to be nasty too. They invite you too to do things differently. Life would be better—though it would be very different at home and at work and even at church—if we all feared God and God alone.

I was shocked when I prepared a sermon once on the fear of the Lord, the fear of God, the fear of Christ. I had not realized what a pervasive idea it is throughout the entire Bible. Look it up if you doubt me.

I appreciate that this talk of 'nasty' Christians is disagreeable. I read an early draft of this chapter as the final lecture of a term and used it to start a discussion of 'life after L'Abri' with the group about to leave. Several of them reacted against the word. They suggested several in its place, including 'uncompromising' and 'courageous'. However, I have decided to stick with 'nasty'. My reasoning is that for very few of us does this word have any positive connotations. It has plenty of negative associations, but when we look in the 'positive' bin we see that it is empty. This means that we are free to put new ideas into that container.

If we use words such as 'uncompromising' or 'courageous', they already have good connotations. The 'positive' bin already has things in it. I am not as free to rethink and change my

---

[22] Matthew 10:34
[23] See his argument in Romans 6.
[24] Matthew 10:28

behaviour so that it is more in keeping with what God desires.
I am more likely to fall back into meeting the expectations of
others if I keep reminding myself to be 'uncompromising'. Plenty
of people perhaps have urged me not to compromise or to be
courageous, but no one at church has ever encouraged me to be
nasty. When talking to a generation that is suspicious and weary
of words, you have to use words very carefully and sparingly and
imaginatively.

However, a weightier criticism of this concept was offered
that afternoon. Someone suspected that calling yourself a nasty
Christian might really only be a cover-up for learning to give
full rein to your selfishness. A person could return home to
family, school, work or church and justify their confident self-
centredness by saying they had learned at L'Abri to be 'a nasty
Christian'. That would be a tragedy, because it is precisely the
opposite of what we intend. When a person begins to live in the
fear of the Lord rather than in fear of others—really live this way,
rather than merely talking about it—they may at times appear
selfish to those living around them. They no longer play by the
usual rules. They no longer co-operate with evil, even when it is
presented as something good and respectable and familiar.

Holiness can be very disconcerting that way. But a person
who fears God and God alone is not thereby rendered selfish.
They may actually become very giving of themselves after the
example of this God. They may, in fact, be the one person in the
room who finds time for the person everyone else has written
off. They may speak very kindly—but this is in order to be kind,
not to buy your approval, or to make you like them, or to hide
the fact that in reality they are very angry with you.

Not only had I been ignorant of how pervasive is the concept
of fearing God and God alone, I had been uncomfortable with
it. It seemed the antithesis to love and intimacy and fellowship.
But I found that it was linked to all of these and more. It is when
we fear God and God alone that we can be honest with others
and invite them to be honest with us. It is when we fear God

and God alone that he reveals himself to us.[25] It is when we fear
God and God alone that we can do the right thing in difficult
circumstances and can face the uncertainty of a grim future. I
don't do this well. I still fear other people and their expectations.
I fear my circumstances. But in those rare times when I choose
to fear God instead—a choice that is very closely related to
trusting him—I find myself free to love and serve others. It is
counter-intuitive, and our societies appear to know little about
it. We must try to help our churches to remember the lesson.

Many 'seedlings' have left L'Abri over the past 50 years, and they
have gone on to flourish. I meet them now and then; sometimes
they write. They do it often enough to keep us encouraged that
our efforts are not in vain. The point of the parable of the sower,
however, is that not all do survive. Not all continue and grow in
the grace of the Living God.[26] And some day L'Abri too will pass
away. Only the invisible Church, through which the Spirit of
God blows like a wind, will survive until the Lord Jesus returns
and the curse is lifted. When Schaeffer set up L'Abri, he tried to
make it so dependent on God's provision that it would go extinct
when God stopped supernaturally caring for it. When will this
occur? I don't know.

In John 4, Jesus tells his followers to look at the fields that
are ripe for harvest. Too much of the evangelical church seems
to interpret these words as a promise to the church throughout
history and for all time—as if any field we find will always be
ripe for harvest. I am embarrassed to admit how very recently I
noticed that the passage leans in a very different direction. Jesus
was telling his followers that they were about to do work in their
society that would bring in a great harvest. However, he was also
saying that they would be reaping a crop for which others had
done the hard labour.

[25] For just one example of this surprising dynamic see Psalm 25.
[26] Matthew 13:3–23

The Messiah also told these same disciples that he was sending them out like sheep among wolves.[27] This doesn't sound as triumphant as the harvesting. Our task as his servants is to be faithful in our day whether it is a day of reaping or of sowing. Certainly in Europe today the fields look mostly barren. It is a time for sowing and we must be faithful. It is not wrong to admit that we would rather be living at harvest-time, but when we fear God and God alone we can afford to be honest. North America is, of course, a very different situation: percentages of the population there go to church and claim to believe in Jesus that are beyond the dreams of Europeans. However, I think that Americans need to be very careful. What appears as strength is not always so. America must not trust in her many chariots.[28]

Schaeffer apparently thought that his most important book was *True Spirituality*. The story goes that the book was largely born out of his experience of a late-night conversation with two women, to whom he was speaking passionately about the freedom found in Christ. It was only late in the conversation that he realized that these women needed a different message. He was convinced that they were in danger of using their freedom in Christ in a false way.

It is just possible that L'Abri is similarly late in a conversation with Western culture. We have encouraged our students to be people of their day, to engage in its arts and sciences and institutions in recognition of the Lordship of Christ over all of life. We have watched the movies, walked the galleries of the museums and read the prize-winning novels. We have spoken out against the sacred/secular dichotomy that values certain kinds of human activity as more spiritual than others. We have urged those who believe in the Bible to be active politically and to co-operate with others for just laws protecting unborn people. These are themes of L'Abri that have contributed beauty to many

[27] Matthew 10:16
[28] 2 Kings 19:23

lives over the years, and these themes remain true, just as what
Schaeffer was saying about freedom in Christ was true.

It was on just such themes that I was invited to speak to a
small congregation from a university city in Hungary. They were
going away for their annual summer camp to the *puszta*, a desert
in the centre of that country that I had been wholly unaware
existed. It is here that the winds that blow over the steppes of
Eastern Europe lose their energy and so drop their load of sand.
The topic for the week was 'In the world but not of the world'. It
was an ideal opportunity to encourage this church, which had
cellists and opera singers and ceramicists and businesspeople,
that they should be involved in building their society and
creating their culture with their many skills.

On the Friday morning, near the end of the week, my topic
was to be 'Living in the world as God's separate people'. I had
brought with me the outlines of a lecture on the lordship of
Christ over all of life, over all of life, but if I didn't tell them its
original title they would never know.

I rarely use the language that I am about to—it is so
subjective, and it is not open to investigation by the reader. But
that Thursday night, in my little room overlooking a farmyard,
I felt no peace at all as I considered the material I was going to
give the next morning. It was what we had been saying for years,
and it had helped so many people to understand how to live
before God in the world; but that night I was far beyond 'having
no peace'—I was positively in turmoil. The hours were swept
away by the hands of my alarm clock. I sat on the floor writing
outline after outline until my bed was almost covered with
crumpled paper.

I began fidgeting. For the first time in years of public
speaking, I was seriously envisaging standing before rows of
expectant faces the next morning and saying, 'I'm sorry, but I
have nothing to say to you on this topic.' They had flown me at
great cost all the way from England, and was I going to give them
nothing to discuss and wrestle with? (Because, being Hungarians

and therefore very earnest, they would talk for hours together about what I said in a lecture. They were careful not simply to agree without shaking my thoughts and seeing what fell out of their pockets.) I prayed and sweated. I opened my Bible and began poring over the New Testament. I had no passage in mind; nothing seemed to fit these people as I had grown to know them and their situation.

It was getting very late and my panic was far advanced when I came upon 2 Corinthians 6:14–7:1, a passage that might have been obvious to everyone else but was far from obvious to me. I was terrified at what I was to explain, and yet I felt a profound peace as I confronted it that went deeper than mere relief at not having to lose face in front of an audience.

> Do not be yoked together with unbelievers.

This is not a very promising beginning. Paul then goes on to ask five rhetorical questions—questions whose answers are already obvious to both author and reader.

> For what do righteousness and wickedness have in common?

Nothing. The two are in bitter competition and are not partners. They are going in different directions. They hope for different things.

> Or what fellowship can light have with darkness?

None. Only one can be present at a time. They do not mix; they do not *commune* in fellowship.

> What harmony is there between Christ and Belial?

None—even if they are bound together as two strings on the same instrument. Together they make a discordant noise. They are not in tune with each other. Christ does not share any purpose with other gods. It should set your teeth on edge to hear them played at the same time.

The questions fall like hammer blows. The heaviest falls next, a blow I don't want to acknowledge.

> What does a believer have in common with an unbeliever?

I wanted to say: 'A lot, in every respect.' I wanted to talk about how we share together in a common world. We both love our children and worry about them. When there is a drought, the crops of both of us die. We both appreciate the song of a blackbird sitting on the garden wall. We both need love and hope but cannot manufacture our own. Both of us have to work in a world of toil. Neither of us live perfectly according to what we believe is true about the cosmos.

But it is a rhetorical question. The answer is: nothing. Nothing is shared. We have nothing in common.

> What agreement is there between the temple of God and idols?

I wanted to point out how incorrigibly religious human beings are and how we all seek something transcendent as a source of identity, meaning and purpose. Everyone seeks spiritual significance, even if they believe they have no spirit. I wanted to argue that Christians can have non-Christian friends and that we do not have to seize power and do away with the infidels.

But it is a rhetorical question and the answer is 'There is no agreement.' The two are implacable foes. Their worshippers may be able to share a *polis*, but the two cannot share the same space in a person's heart.

And then Paul quotes some Old Testament promises, sandwiched between the credits 'As God has said' and 'says the Lord Almighty':

> For we are the temple of the living God. As God has said: 'I will live with them and walk among them, and I will be their God, and they will be my people.'

> 'Therefore come out from them
>     and be separate, says the Lord.
> Touch no unclean thing,
>     and I will receive you.'
> 'I will be a Father to you,
>     and you will be my sons and daughters,
>         says the Lord Almighty.'

In the middle of this is mentioned one thing that a Christian does share with an unbeliever: we originate from the same place. We started off where they still stand. For in one sense a Christian is merely a non-Christian who has been reconciled to the Living God. There is nothing special within us about which we can brag or in which we can place confidence. I am not a reconciled non-Christian because I am more intelligent or harder-working. It is because we share so much with unbelievers that we have to come out and be separate. It is possible to forget this, to ignore this, to go on acting as if we are not reconciled and have not been pointed in a very different direction from the one we once faced in.

This sounds very harsh to our ears, but it is actually good news for our generation. Paul is, in fact, agreeing that following this religion is not a matter of words only. It changes things. It demands things of us.

> Since we have these promises, dear friends, let us purify ourselves from everything that contaminates body and spirit, perfecting holiness out of reverence for God.

Schaeffer was correct: some people need to hear about the freedom found in Christ. It is about becoming more and more yourself as you seek to serve the will of your Creator and to accept his generosity. L'Abri has been correct: Christ is Lord over all human endeavour and we are to have the same attitude that Christ did, being servants amid the confusion of messy, everyday life.

The passage about being 'unequally yoked' is one we hear quoted most often about the prospects of a Christian falling in love with an unbeliever and marrying them. It can be applied to that, but it means much more. We who want to follow Jesus Christ, we who desire to fear God and God alone, are not to be joined in such a fashion to anyone who believes that all free actions are acceptable. If they leave the path God wants them to take, we must not be so joined together that we have to leave it with them. Or if, in obedience to God, we ought to leave a path of social convention, we must not be joined in such a way that we are obliged to remain on it because they do.

However, if we find ourselves able to walk along the same path—to provide a better education for our children, or to combat Aids in Africa or to campaign together in a referendum on the European constitution—we are free to do so. It would be perverse not to. Associating with people or being their heartfelt friend or their fellow supporter of a cause is not the same as being joined to them in such a way that we cannot give ultimate obedience to the will of Jesus Christ.

Both messages are true and timely. We must be careful to emphasize the one that we need to hear and that comes to us less naturally, rather than congratulating ourselves and deceiving ourselves into thinking that we are being obedient when actually we are following our own desires and baptizing our own personal preferences.

Does this sound difficult? Schaeffer, I think, would have said it is impossible unless we are walking supernaturally in the very midst of everyday life. It is impossible if we are not walking moment by moment in the wisdom and power of the Holy Spirit.

# Contact Information

For up-to-date information and news about L'Abri Fellowship International, visit www.labri.org

Or contact the individual branches:

**L'Abri Switzerland**

    Chalet Bellevue

    1884 Huémoz

    Switzerland

E-mail: swiss@labri.org

Office tel: +41 24-495-2139

Office fax: +41 24-495-7647

Student tel: +41 24-495-1897

**L'Abri England**

    The Manor House

    Greatham, Liss

    GU33 6HF

    United Kingdom

E-mail: england@labri.org

Office tel: +44 1420-538436

Office fax: +44 1420-538432

Student tel: +44 1420-538329

**L'Abri Holland (Eck en Wiel)**

    Huize Kortenhoeve

    Burgemeester Verbrughweg 40

    4024 HR Eck en Wiel

    The Netherlands

E-mail: labri@labri.nl

Office tel: +31 344-691914

**L'Abri Holland (Utrecht)**

    Kromme Nieuwegracht 90

    3512 HM Utrecht

    The Netherlands

E-mail: wim.rietkerk@labri.nl

Office tel: +31 30-231-6933

**L'Abri Korea**

    50-2 Hooamdong,

    Yongsangu

    Seoul 140-190

    South Korea

E-mail: korea@labri.org

Office tel: +82 2-733-5309

Office fax: +82-2-318-2595

**L'Abri US (Massachusetts)**

    49 Lynbrook Road

    Southborough, MA 01772

    United States of America

E-mail: southborough@labri.org

Office tel: +1 508-481-6490

Office fax: +1 508-460-5021

Student tel: +1 508-481-9101

**L'Abri US (Minnesota)**

    1465 12th Ave NE

    Rochester, MN 55906-4383

    United States of America

E-mail: rochester@labri.org

Office tel: +1 507-536-0108

**L'Abri Sweden**

    Bidevindvagen 4

    S-260 42 Molle

    Sweden

E-mail: sweden@labri.org

Office tel: +46 42-347632

Office fax: +46 42-347832

**L'Abri Australia**

   10 River Road

   Elderslie NSW 2570

   Australia

E-mail:  australia@labri.org

Office tel: +61 2-46-580227 (or local in NSW:  4658 0227)


**L'Abri Canada**

   RR #1 Q-8

   511 Cowan Road

   Bowen Island, BC

   Canada V0N 1G0

E-mail: canadianlabri@shaw.ca

Office tel: +1 604-947-6986

Office fax: +1 604-947-6987


**L'Abri Germany**

   c/o Petra & Andreas Hartmann

   Im Haeg 9

   38474 Tuelau-Voitze

   Germany

E-mail: info@labri.de

Office tel: +49 5833-970882

Office fax: +49 5833-970881

# Also available from

PiQUANT
editions

*www.piquant.net*

### The Complete Works of Hans Rookmaaker (6 vols)
*Edited by Marleen Hengelaar-Rookmaaker*

Set Price: £190.00 ($295.00)
Special student discounts available!

Order from:
Piquant Editions Ltd
PO Box 83
Carlisle CA3 9GR
United Kingdom

E-mail: info@piquant.net

Or buy on-line from: www.abebooks.com

# By Demonstration: God

## *Fifty Years and a Week at L'Abri*

*by Wade Bradshaw*

(ISBN 1-903689-33-3)

**£6.99 / $11.99**

---

Name: _____

Mailing address (including postcode and country): _____

_____

_____

_____

Quantity: ___

---

Name: _____

Mailing address (including postcode and country): _____

_____

_____

_____

Quantity: ___

---

**See reverse for shipping costs depending on ship-to country**

Total number of copies ordered: _____    Total shipping cost: _____

Total order value: _____

I enclose a cheque (made payable to Piquant Editions) ☐ /
I will pay by credit card ☐

Please cirlce:   Visa   Mastercard   Switch   Solo

Your credit card number: _____ Security code:_____

Start date: _____   Expiration date: _____

Name of credit card holder: _____

Address of credit card holder: _____

_____

Card holder signature: _____

**PiQUANT**
editions

**Please send completed order forms to:**

Piquant Editions
PO Box 83
Carlisle, CA3 9GR
United Kingdom

*E-mail: info@piquant.net*

**All shipping prices are per address. If sending to multiple addresses treat each address as a separate order.**

Shipping cost for orders being sent to USA:

| Order Value | Low Cost(Post Office) | Standard(Fed Ex) |
|---|---|---|
| Up to $20 | $4 | $6 |
| Up to $50 | $5.50 | $8 |
| Up to $100 | 11% of order value | 16% of order value |
| Over $100 | 9% of order value | 13% of order value |

For orders being sent to Canada please contact **luke.lewis@piquant.net** for a shipping quote

**Shipping cost for orders being sent to the UK and Europe:**

For orders being sent within the UK shipping is £2.95 regardless of quantity

For orders being sent outside the UK shipping is £2.95 plus £2.00 for every copy sent (i.e. £4.95 for one copy, £6.95 for 2 copies...)

**If ordering from outside USA/Canada and UK/Europe please order from**

**www.abebooks.com**